PRAISE FOR
NEW STARTUP MINDSET

"Sandra Shpilberg is a unicorn and this book is one, too. Simultaneously profound and practical, replete with the soundest advice and great storytelling while being tender toward the reader's soul, this is a game-changing must-read for anyone who dreams of creating a business—and in particular for those who don't fit the mold. Go Sandra Shpilberg, go!"

—Julie Lythcott-Haims, author of the *New York Times* bestseller *How to Raise an Adult,* and *Real American: A Memoir*

"Sandra Shpilberg's phenomenal book, which showcases her literary talent and entrepreneurial skills, will change the minds of aspiring entrepreneurs . . . for the better."

—Michael Szenberg, editor in chief emeritus, *American Economist*; distinguished professor of economics, Touro College and University System

"Sandra Shpilberg's book is a must-read for all founders or anyone contemplating starting a business. She graciously provides an insider's guide on how to overcome a wide array of challenges that founders face. This is a gem of a resource for any type of entrepreneur."

—Mona Bijoor, founder of JOOR, partner of Kings Circle Capital, author of *Startups and Downs: The Secrets of Resilient Entrepreneurs*

"If you're thinking about starting a business, *New Startup Mindset* is THE book to read. Sandra's story offers lots of practical wisdom and inspiring examples delivered with even more heart. It's the book I was looking for during my early days of running CD Baby—this new way of thinking would have had me jumping out of my seat in excitement."

—Derek Sivers, founder of CD Baby
and author of *Anything You Want*

"Perfectionism and fear can be big internal stumbling blocks for entrepreneurs, especially women and minorities. *New Startup Mindset* offers insights that can transform your journey and enable you to build a successful company on your terms. A must-read for anyone who wishes to lead the creation of a company."

—Sally Helgesen, author of *How Women Rise*
and *The Female Vision*

NEW STARTUP MINDSET

NEW STARTUP MINDSET

Ten Mindset Shifts to Build the Company of Your Dreams

SANDRA SHPILBERG

GIRL FRIDAY BOOKS

GFB GIRL FRIDAY BOOKS

Published by Girl Friday Books™, Seattle

Produced by Girl Friday Productions
www.girlfridayproductions.com

Design: Paul Barrett
Project management: Bethany Davis

Image credits: cover © Shutterstock/Rzoog

ISBN (paperback): 978-1-954854-04-8
ISBN (e-book): 978-1-954854-08-6
ISBN (audiobook): 978-1-954854-09-3

Library of Congress Control Number: 2021906238

Second edition

To Coby and Karina.
When we first moved to Palo Alto,
I said you were adaptive and resilient.
You responded: "Are we adopted and Brazilian!?"
You are, and will always be,
my most meaningful and loved co-creations.

When you learn, teach.
When you get, give.

—Maya Angelou

CONTENTS

PART 1: START

Chapter 1: Beginner's Mindset

Chapter 2: Single Deep Focus

PART 2: BUILD

Chapter 3: The Flow Is Forward

Chapter 9: Your Best Effort Is Never Burnout

PART 3: EXIT

Chapter 10: Ask for the Really Good Stuff (and You Deserve It)

NEW STARTUP MINDSET
CAN HELP YOU IF . . .

- You want to start something new but are afraid to do so
- You want to start something new but are waiting for X, Y, and Z to happen first
- You are afraid of hard work or burnout
- You are afraid startup culture is not for you
- You can't (even) imagine yourself raising funds from venture capitalists
- You seek financial freedom
- You seek inner freedom
- You seek meaning in your life

FOREWORD

In *New Startup Mindset*, Sandra Shpilberg, founder and CEO of Seeker Health, lays out a clear path that all business owners should take: solve a true problem, delight your employees and customers, do it sustainably and profitably. It's a model that's easy to understand and based on tried and true business principles that will change the way you approach your business and your life.

Shpilberg introduces us to a new way of thinking about starting and scaling a successful company. She illustrates that Silicon Valley's startup formula is *not the only* beacon for success. Investing in predominantly white, male founders (in 2020, female founder funding declined from 2.8% to 2.3%) and pushing capital into businesses without sustainable results yet—all in the name of creating a "unicorn"—is a model that only works for a select few companies. As a result, that formula propagates false hope and incorrect lessons for the next generation of entrepreneurs.

Now more than ever, the world needs innovative entrepreneurs, and Shpilberg's model is an essential formula for how to be one. The pandemic helped many of us crystallize our priorities in business and in life. Today, it's not just about creating a business that inspires people to consume, it's about building a sustainable business that tackles big problems such as climate change, health care, and education. Entrepreneurship offers a path to innovation that can make the most meaningful impact.

Through this book, you will also gain a realistic view of entrepreneurship that is neither linear nor about the final outcome. Success will always take more steps than you expected or planned, and that's something I highlighted in my own book, *Startups and Downs: The Secrets of Resilient Entrepreneurs*.

Most entrepreneurs, however, don't initially think about the *real* law of progression. They create a big vision and aim to reach their goals in a few (difficult) steps—and that rarely works. Landing a large batch of funding can be thrilling, but it might not be what your business truly needs at that moment. When you rush the process, it may feel like you've succeeded in the short-term, but your long-term approach suffers.

As the well-known self-help author Robert Collier once said, "Success is the sum of small efforts, repeated day in and day out." Consistency and purposeful actions should drive the processes that you utilize to work. Through this iterative approach, you take steps to achieve your vision.

As an entrepreneur, whether you find yourself moving backward, forward, or pivoting, having consistent and clear focus will lead to progress. Even failure is progress if you can make the most of what you've learned. The trick is keeping your eyes trained on your goal. Sustained momentum is what brings actual results.

By picking up this book, you will have access to the type of eye-opening inspiration that is the seedling for entrepreneurship. You, too, can create a company that makes an impact, and *New Startup Mindset* will show you how.

Mona Bijoor
Founder, JOOR
Partner, Kings Circle Capital
Author, *Startups and Downs: The Secrets of Resilient Entrepreneurs*
May 2021

THE FORMULA
IS BROKEN

What's normal? A setting on a washing machine.
—Ashley Purdy

If this is a man's world, who cares?
—Sophia Amoruso, Nasty Gal

The formula: Young male founder in a garage in Silicon Valley. He's Caucasian, Indian, or Asian, and a programmer. He has a cofounder in the same demographic. He's accepted into that fancy name incubator, where he spends three months focusing on how to turn his idea into a business and learning how to pitch for venture capital. He receives incubator and angel funds and spends the next year attempting to figure out how to prove traction.

If he only had more funding, he thinks.

He pitches to venture capitalists (VCs). He drops into the conversation that he was indeed number one in his ninth-grade class, and "Top 20 under 20" because #humblebrag. Then, based on untethered optimism and a fictitious valuation, not rooted in the fundamentals of business—that is, revenue and profit—he closes his Series A of funding. *TechCrunch* writes about him, and the hype circus is now open for business.

He's exhausted from the fundraising round, but he uses whatever adrenaline he can muster to build the company. He hires a team of programmers and some equally expensive "adults in the room." He leases a shiny office in San Francisco, with a view of a lit-up suspension bridge and an endless smorgasbord of free food. Even though there's a business to build, he devotes most of his time to fundraising—every round gets more tech press coverage and increases the fictional valuation.

His father posts the article on Facebook—the one that says his company is valued at $10 million! This gives him just about all the satisfaction he'll ever need to know that he's made it. His ego dances. This is the pinnacle. Never mind that there aren't any customers paying for anything, and the company is now losing $3 million this year alone.

He knows that every fundraising round dilutes his stake in the company, but he chalks up this math to the name of the game—the formula for startups—the way to build a new company. After all, with these VC names on his investor list, he's surely bound for success.

Until the customers don't show up, or don't stay, and the VCs stop coming to board meetings. The company limps along for another two years, spending investors' money. He looks back at those *TechCrunch* articles he's printed in a tiny font and put in his wallet. The real writing, though, is on the wall—you need paying customers—but he's not going to read it, because what he needs is another round of funding.

If he only had more funding, then his dream would come true: to be in the 0.05 percent of startups for whom investors still show up to board meetings, eventually take the company public, liquidate equity via an IPO, and transfer the ongoing losses of the company to the public markets.

I'M HERE TO TELL YOU THAT THIS FORMULA IS BROKEN. This formula is broken because it disregards real results such as revenue and profit, and puts excessive emphasis on hype and improbable outsized outcomes. This formula is in itself a limiting belief, which on a daily basis stops many creators from starting and building companies.

THERE'S ANOTHER WAY TO CREATE COMPANIES THAT MAKE AN IMPACT. From 2015 to 2018, I led my company, Seeker Health, from nothing at all to a leading patient-finding platform that served forty-plus biotechnology customers, doubled revenue, and tripled profit each year. We connected millions of patients with serious conditions to clinical trials for investigational treatments. In 2018, my startup was acquired by a large life science services conglomerate.

During this entrepreneurial pursuit, I did almost everything differently than the traditional path: I chose to be a solo founder. I didn't pursue an incubator. I didn't accept outside funding from angel investors or venture capitalists. I charged customers from day one for work they found valuable. I led the development of software even though I wasn't a programmer. I hired the smallest possible team, and let the "machine," the software we built to achieve automation, scale us. Our office was the size of a walk-in closet at a coworking space, and instead of free food we preferred work-from-home Fridays. Instead of fictitious valuations, I booked revenue and profit—the basic measures of any business that's meant to continue and thrive. Instead of smoke and mirrors, hype and ego, I focused exclusively on acquiring paying customers and improving the way we served them.

Oh, and I almost forgot to label myself: I'm a woman, an immigrant from Uruguay, a mother of two school-aged children, and a person who needs eight hours of sleep each day.

I'm on the other side of this journey now, and you deserve to know how you too can chuck the formula, adopt the new startup mindset, and build the company of your dreams. Before we begin our journey, allow me to dispel a few toxic myths about startups. These myths originate from the broken formula and are so limiting, so damaging, so injurious to entrepreneurship that I must address them now. If not, these myths may pop into your mind, like a game of whack-a-mole, to impede your forward progress. So, let's go through them, and promise me that if they pop up for you later in the reading, you will whack them, like the ugly, despicable pests that they are.

SEVEN STARTUP MYTHS WE NEED TO DISPEL NOW

MYTH 1: UNICORN OR NOTHING.

Of all myths of startup life, I begin with the most dangerous one: the belief that unless you've created a Facebook or a Google, you and your company are nothing. This couldn't be further from the truth. A unicorn is a startup with a valuation of $1 billion or higher. The term was coined in 2013 by venture capitalist Aileen Lee, who chose a mythical animal to represent the statistical rarity of such a venture. Go ahead and have ambitious goals, but know that many companies make a great impact without becoming unicorns. Right under unicorns, you'll find lions, giraffes, horses, gazelles, and all sorts of valuable, real, and well-fed animals.

MYTH 2: YOU ARE YOUR STARTUP.

No, you are not. You are a human being trying to have a meaningful life on this planet for the impermanent period of time that is afforded by your body. You may spend three, five, ten, or twenty years of your life working on your company, which may live beyond you, or may not. The startup is not you, and you are not your startup. This is an important myth to dispel early, because should your startup die, it will not mean that you do as well.

MYTH 3: YOU NEED A COFOUNDER.
You don't need a cofounder, and in fact having a cofounder may affect the ability of your company to succeed. Research shows that companies started by solo founders survive longer than those started by teams. In addition, organizations started by solo founders generate more revenue than organizations started by founder pairs.[1] Thus, forget waiting for a cofounder and trying cofounder dating. You are all of the founding power your startup will ever need.

MYTH 4: HARDER WORK MEANS BIGGER SUCCESS.
Better work means bigger success, and better work is not measured in hours. Better work is measured in quality and effectiveness. I can spend eighty hours cold-calling a list of customers who will never give me the time of day, or I can spend five hours having focused one-hour meetings with five targeted and engaged potential customers. The first eighty hours of cold-calling are likely to yield zero revenue for my startup. The five hours of targeted meetings are likely to yield at least $500,000 revenue for my startup, and save me a lot of frustration. Don't work longer; work better.

---

1. Jason Greenberg and Ethan R. Mollick, "Sole Survivors: Solo Ventures Versus Founding Teams," *SSRN* (January 23, 2018): http://dx.doi.org/10.2139/ssrn.3107898.

MYTH 5: I NEED VENTURE CAPITALISTS TO FUND MY STARTUP.
There are many alternatives to funding a startup, and I'll spend time in chapter 4 sharing my thoughts on this topic. I built my startup on customer revenue and took zero outside funding. By the time Seeker Health was acquired, I was still the sole owner. From a personal finance perspective, consider that you can own 2 percent of an unlikely unicorn and get paid last, should a liquidation event occur. Or you can own 100 percent of a gazelle and get paid first. The bottom line is that some businesses need VC, but many do not. For the businesses that need VC, investors are looking for companies with some traction, so either way, in the early stages of your startup, you're likely to have to find a way to operate it, grow it, and prove traction without VC.

MYTH 6: I NEED TO BE A YOUNG WHITE MAN TO BE SUCCESSFUL AS A STARTUP FOUNDER.
Nope. Despite the popular image of a college dropout as a successful founder, the average age of successful founders is forty-five, and older founders outperform their younger colleagues.[2] If you don't see people who look like you starting and building companies, this is of no consequence to your journey. There's only one you, and what you can create is important. If you have to blaze a path, then do it: for you and for the people like you who are right behind you. Ditch the labels (all of them) and go do it.

MYTH 7: MY STARTUP NEEDS LUCK.
We make our own luck. There are many things we do not control in life, but we can control how we show up, work effectively, create, and build. You'll be relying on your skills, focus,

---

2. Pierre Azoulay et al. "Research: The Average Age of a Successful Startup Founder Is 45," *Harvard Business Review*, July 11, 2018, https://hbr.org/2018/07/research-the-average-age-of-a-successful-startup-founder-is-45.

work ethic, connections, and ability to rest and regenerate. "Bad luck" or "failures" are useful data for redirection. This element we call "luck" is simply life redirecting you to where you will create your best work. You can't summon luck to work for you, but you can instead summon your skills, focus, and mindfulness, and direct them toward your creation.

Now, I'm mindful of the fact that you might benefit from some context to understand my obstacles, appreciate my triumphs, and identify my biases.

So let's play the Authentic Relating game called "If you really knew me." It goes like this: We pair up, it's you and me, and we'll take turns. I'll start each sentence with the phrase "If you really knew me, you would know . . ." At the two-minute mark, we'll switch roles.

Here I go:

IF YOU REALLY KNEW ME, YOU WOULD KNOW . . .
I was born in Uruguay, that tiny country in South America nestled between the two giants, Argentina and Brazil. My grandparents escaped the Holocaust in Poland and Romania, and the transatlantic ships that saved their lives took them to a country no one had ever heard of.

IF YOU REALLY KNEW ME, YOU WOULD KNOW . . .
In Uruguay, my father had two small businesses—a hardware store and a furniture-making facility—and my mother worked as a financial advisor at a bank. These three incomes didn't amount to abundance, and so my father's dream was to move our family to a more workaholic—I mean, *productive* country. He dreamed big and far, and always legally.

IF YOU REALLY KNEW ME, YOU WOULD KNOW . . .

I have two younger brothers I really adore, and this is important because since the age of three, I've been telling boys what to do.

IF YOU REALLY KNEW ME, YOU WOULD KNOW . . .

In 1992, when I was sixteen years old, my family and I legally immigrated to the United States. With green cards in hand, but lacking in winter coats and English vocabulary, we landed in Brooklyn, New York, on the coldest, grayest, and saddest day ever recorded in the history of humankind. Leaving everything and everyone I knew behind made for one of the most powerful, formative experiences of my life: I learned to hustle, go on, and survive, while feeling pain.

IF YOU REALLY KNEW ME, YOU WOULD KNOW . . .

My family was much poorer in America, "the land of opportunity," than we had ever been in Uruguay. On my first day of school, I received a thick pad of red raffle tickets. Puzzled, I asked what they were. "Free food," said the office manager. My parents' income was so nonexistent that I qualified for free breakfast and lunch at school.

IF YOU REALLY KNEW ME, YOU WOULD KNOW . . .

I am (was?) very Type A. During my formative years, I cried when I got a 98 on a test, because I only liked grades with three digits. I love to-do lists and efficiency. This inclination has served me rather well. I'm the first person in my family to graduate from college, earn a graduate degree at an Ivy League school, start a company, get that company acquired, achieve financial independence, go to therapy to "feel my feelings," find mindfulness to deal with stress, and punch fear in its ugly face.

IF YOU REALLY KNEW ME, YOU WOULD KNOW . . .
I married my high school sweetheart, also an immigrant and entrepreneur. This relatively stable relationship has been foundational in the pursuit of unstable income sources. Lovingly, we produced two children, who appear to tolerate business talk at the dinner table without anaphylactic reactions.

IF YOU REALLY KNEW ME, YOU WOULD KNOW . . .
My life began to take off, to feel full and free, when I changed my mindset. I'd like to show you these mindset shifts I used so you can choose to change yours.

OK, my two minutes are way up.

Note to you: It feels amazing to share authentically, and I love to get to know my readers better. Use your turn to make use of your two minutes of authentic relating by visiting my website, sandrashpilberg.com/know, to find a space to share, anonymously or not.

WHY THIS BOOK, *NEW STARTUP MINDSET*?
A mindset is the established set of attitudes you hold. Whether you are aware of it or not, your mindset affects everything you do and how you do it. A startup is a company in its first stages of operations. At this point, a startup is often confirming product/market fit, hiring the first set of employees, and securing the resources needed to build and grow. Most important, a startup is trying to live and not die. The mindset with which you approach the process of starting and building a company is fundamental to its success.

I wrote this book to introduce you to a new mindset for starting and building a company that makes an impact. I also wrote this book to help you dispel toxic startup myths about what it takes to create a company that provides value. Extreme lack and extreme excess both come at a cost, and so I'm inviting you to consider a middle path.

This book is written for creators—those with the desire, guts, and stamina to start something that didn't exist before, and build it for maximum impact. Your creation may be a company, a book, a movie, a class, or an empire. Whatever your dream, the mindset shifts described in this book are your road map for periods of high output.

New Startup Mindset is about finding this middle path, where you can create from a place that's intentional and aligned with your core values; where instead of following the blazed path just because it's there, you craft the path that makes sense in your mind, heart, and body for your creation. There is no use in waiting for a better moment than this one, and *New Startup Mindset* is about encouraging your creation now. *New Startup Mindset* is about delivering meaningful value to your customers, your employees, yourself, and anyone your business touches. **New Startup Mindset is meant to set you free.**

HOW THIS BOOK IS ORGANIZED

The book's three parts correspond to the startup cycle.

Part 1, START, is where I focus on how to create something where there was once nothing. These first steps are leaps into the unknown, and as such require mindset shifts to summon the needed courage.

Part 2, BUILD, is where I focus on how to grow the company. These next few steps are marathonic in nature and require stamina, grit, and the ability to get up after tripping on hurdles.

Part 3 is EXIT, a jargony business word to describe a positive end for your role in the startup. You can continue to run your startup until the day you die, but most founders prefer to find a suitable and planned end to their role. This exit may take the form of another company coming along to purchase the value created, an IPO, or other mechanisms. There's incredible richness in finding the right end. In this part, I share the process I went through to evaluate offers from potential acquirers of Seeker Health.

Each chapter begins with a tale from the trenches, in which I share a part of the story of building Seeker Health. While my story is just that—one story—I share it to give you a view into my process, thoughts, and feelings in the hope that they may serve as a mirror to your experience, or an opportunity to see things turn out differently.

Next, I offer a teaching designed to enable a mindset shift. The teachings are primarily based on my direct experiences, which will differ from yours. I've added evidence-based research to support many of the teachings.

Each chapter contains a guided meditation to help you visualize and internalize the proposed mindset shifts. For these, it's best to imagine a meditation teacher, such as Tara Brach or Jack Kornfield, reading them out loud to you in their soothing voices. Each chapter closes with a TL;DR (too long; didn't read) summary for busy creators like yourself.

To maintain confidentiality and protect the privacy of certain companies and persons, I've changed some names and identifying features.

I wrote the tales to match the chronological order in which they took place, and you may read them sequentially. You may also choose to read any chapter in any order you please. Stay mindful as to why that chapter attracts your attention in the present moment over others. Wisdom rests in being aware of what attracts and repels you in the present moment.

FINALLY, TWO THINGS I FEEL ARE NECESSARY.
First, allow me to check my privilege at the door. The color of my skin is white. I've had access to excellent formal and informal education. I've been employed my entire adult life.

I've never experienced real hunger, unless it was self-inflicted. I always had a roof over my head. Phil was working, and I had money in my bank account when I started Seeker Health.

Last, grant me the opportunity to state my humility. This is my take, at this time, on a new mindset for entrepreneurship. It's different enough from the formula that it's worth sharing. I don't know it all. I'm still learning.

OK, I'm ready. Are you?

Let's get this startup started.

PART 1

START

CHAPTER 1

BEGINNER'S MINDSET

Don't be intimidated by what you don't know.
That can be your greatest strength and ensure
that you do things differently from everyone else.
—Sara Blakely, founder and CEO, Spanx

TALE FROM THE TRENCHES

"When did this start?" the doctor asked. I thought of what to say, because beginnings are not always clear. Did it start when I lost my voice? When that guy sneezed on me in seat 18A, or when I got on the plane? Or was I already feeling a tingle in my throat before all of this?

Pinpointing the beginning of when I caught the entrepreneurial bug feels just about the same way. Was the beginning when I lay awake sleepless at night as an employee of BioMarin, pondering how to find patients for rare-disease treatments? Or was it when I woke up to realize I had an actual dream in which I ran a company that accelerated the finding of patients? Or was it in the late 1990s, when I pitched a Spanish-language marketplace to a room of angel investors who told me to go grow up? Was it when I was my father's helper at his tiny hardware store in Uruguay, before I even spoke English, and when he taught me how to delight customers, even if all they were buying was ten feet of white cable? Maybe it was even much earlier than that, when I was six years old, and the teacher asked me what I wanted to do when I grew up. I answered: "When I grow up, I want to tell people what to do," not yet having the language to say anything more sophisticated, like *I want to be a founder, a leader, an executive, or whoever else tells people what to do.*

The closest I can take you to the germination of the seed that became Seeker Health is November of 2015. I was working at Nora Therapeutics, a startup biotech company, as VP of strategic marketing and commercial planning, and preparing for a potential launch of a new treatment in recurrent miscarriage.

The treatment was still in clinical trials, which are research experiments performed on humans under very controlled circumstances to produce the clinical data necessary for approval from regulatory agencies, like the FDA. The Nora team was working hard to enroll participants in the trial as quickly as possible. Each month of trial operations amounted to a very significant cash burn. Nora had raised funds from five venture capital firms, but by the time I joined, the company was in its last year of runway, that is, the time until the money in the bank runs out. While clinical trial sites struggled to find all of the participants required, I instinctively knew that women with recurrent miscarriages were online, and specifically on Facebook.

Miscarriages are not fun. I had one myself in 2006 and had learned from that experience about the potent stigma. Most miscarriages are nothing more than the body doing the natural selection job of rejecting a defective embryo. However, women with miscarriages often feel guilty, depressed, lonely, and mute. Talking about their miscarriages with their families or best friends is a loaded topic: What if Grandma-to-Be despairs at the possibility of no offspring to take on the family name? What if even one's BFFs think a miscarriage is "contagious"? And so, these women turn to Facebook to find strangers in groups and community pages to offer support, empathy, and information.

Given the very personal insight I had on this specific population, I began working with the VP of clinical operations to develop an awareness campaign to reach this audience. Back then, we couldn't quite locate service providers that would help us with the strategies I wanted to execute, such as optimizing a compliant campaign on Facebook, or creating an online prescreening tool that could securely handle private patient information. I began to piece this project together, and at the height of the campaign, we had ninety women signing up every month to be considered for participation. Nora Therapeutics needed only another 150 participants. In a matter of months, the study was enrolled.

I recall sitting in a board meeting with the Nora team, VCs, and independent directors to review the company's status. After we shared the trial enrollment progress, one of the VC directors said, "This worked so well, maybe we should become a digital marketing company of some kind." People laughed and dismissed the comment. I, on the other hand, held on to that compliment for a while, fantasizing about all the companies like Nora that could benefit from a real end-to-end patient-finding platform—not the patchwork we had just cobbled together. With the trial now enrolled, it was time to wait for the data.

Around this time my father, my original and true source of unconditional love, passed away. He had been battling several conditions for a decade and had formed an unusual pattern of spending several weeks in the hospital, often in intensive care, and then emerging for several months, even years of health. This last time in the ICU, he didn't emerge. As I grieved over his passing, I also realized that health had left him before he had a chance to realize his own dream of starting a business in the United States. As immigrants, my parents worked for employers ... the more stable, the better. This open action item of my father's dream to start a business gnawed at me—almost poking me in his voice: *"Sandrita, you do it for us?"*

A few months later, once the clinical trial was completed and the data interpreted, Nora Therapeutics decided not to continue the treatment's development.

I was out of a job, and into a great idea for starting a company.

On November 3, 2015, instead of emailing recruiters or polishing my résumé, I pointed my browser to Legalzoom.com, navigated to "Business Formation," and clicked on "Limited Liability Company (LLC)." I entered "Seeker Health."

Where did this name come from? In the evenings leading up to this moment, I was reading Harry Potter to my daughter at bedtime, and we came upon that part in which Harry is chosen as Seeker, an important position in the wizarding sport of Quidditch. The goal of the Seeker is to catch the Golden Snitch. Seekers play a crucial role in Quidditch, as the game does not end until the Seeker catches the Snitch.

The parallels of Quidditch to clinical trials in rare diseases are uncanny. This company I was about to create would play the position of Seeker, trying to find the precious Golden Snitches that are patients with rare diseases. The clinical trial does not end, the data does not get collected, and the treatment cannot be filed for regulatory approval, until the Seeker enrolls patients for the trials.

Beyond geeking out on Harry Potter, the word "Seeker" described me: a Seeker is what I've always been, seeking knowledge, wisdom, freedom, purpose, and impact, and the path to these.

Next, I set my intentions:

- Start and build a company that accelerates the development of important treatments by using technology.
- Learn how to start and build a company.
- Realize the entrepreneurial potential that resided within me, for the benefit of patients and my own family.

With the LLC documents filed and my intentions set, I moved on to define our offering, create a website, and update my colleagues. To design the logo, I hired the most detail-oriented, cheapest graphic designer I knew: my son, then twelve years old. I paid him thirty dollars for his work, and the logo he created for Seeker Health is still used to this day.

From the start, I focused the company on developing digital ad campaigns on social media for clinical trials. This required no significant investment of financial capital, and I was confident I could find at least a few customers willing to give it a try. To learn Facebook advertising, I consulted the most proficient performance digital marketer I knew: my husband. Phil was running a mobile games user acquisition agency that relied on social advertising and data analytics. No one better to show me the ropes and give me some practice assignments, all for free.

Though I had worked in the biotechnology industry for decades by then, every aspect of starting Seeker Health made me feel like a beginner. Until this moment, I had never incorporated a business, developed a software product, or filed a patent. I'd never hired every single team member, let alone been the person each of these employees looked to for decisions, motivation, and culture. I realized that after decades of feeling that I was becoming an expert in biotech commercial and drug development, I was finally . . . a beginner!?

Day after day, I showed up to be a beginner at my startup. But quite soon, I came to the realization that this beginner's mindset was exactly what was propelling me and Seeker

Health forward. As a beginner, instead of judging my lack of experience, I acknowledged my newness to leverage the curiosity, humility, and patience that such a status bestows.

I know now that if I had known more then, I would've never started my company. If I had known more, I would've been able to see the challenges way in advance, when there was still time to turn away. If I had known more, I might have predicted how competitive this market would become, and turned away. And that would have been a huge mistake.

I know now that once I started, the business itself showed me the way.

THE TEACHING: CULTIVATE A BEGINNER'S MINDSET

The beginner's mindset is about approaching all that comes your way with the curiosity, humility, and patience of a person who is engaging with this task for the very first time. Why is the beginner's mindset a productive way to start and build something?

- **A beginner is curious.** Albert Einstein once said, "I have no special talent. I am only passionately curious." A beginner is comfortable with this strong desire to know and learn.
- **A beginner is humble.** Being a beginner absolves you from any delusion of self-importance. A beginner approaches tasks with the reverence and respect required.
- **A beginner is patient.** A beginner has the capacity to accept delays and suffering without getting overly upset. This tolerance is paramount when trying to build a company, relationship, or anything else that endures.
- **A beginner understands that temporary failure is part of enduring success.** Failure is one of the most effective tools for learning. There . . . you failed. Now you know what doesn't work and can focus on what might.

- **A beginner is free of expectations.** Experts suffer from pressure to live up to expectations from themselves and others. But beginners—we are free! We are free to create and fail, try again, have a detour, and then succeed.
- **A beginner asks for help.** By asking for help, you bring more diversity of thought into your venture than if you rely solely on what you *think* you already know.
- **A beginner can respond to the inner critic.** We all have that voice that tells us we are not good enough. It may feel like a bully lives inside your head in a rent-controlled apartment and won't ever move out. A beginner can evict that bully by reminding it that you are just getting started and are figuring things out.

Ethan Kross of the University of Michigan's Emotion and Self Control Lab, and his colleague Ozlem Ayduk of the University of California, Berkeley, say that "the best intervention may be to respond to its grievances from a detached perspective—almost as if you were another person."[3]

A SIMPLE EXERCISE: WRITE A LETTER TO YOUR INNER CRITIC
Summon your inner critic. Hear the garbage it has to say about you. And then write it a simple letter, which may go like this:

> Inner critic,
>   I hear what you are saying, that (insert your name) is (insert X, Y, and Z negative self-talk here), and can't possibly be able to do (insert A, B, C goals and dreams).

---

3.   Jena E Pincott, "Silencing Your Inner Critic," *Psychology Today* (blog), March 4, 2019, https://www.psychologytoday.com/us/articles/201903/silencing-your -inner-critic.

(Insert your name) is at a point where s/he really wants to leap into creating this new venture, and s/he would really appreciate it if you could give her/him the benefit of the doubt. S/he's just starting out, you know? S/he wants to do this, and s/he trusts s/he will figure out a way.

In the case that you are unable to give her/him the benefit of the doubt, then just shut up completely, about X, Y, Z, and A, B, C, and whatever else you may have to say about (insert your name).

Just shut up. I'll reach back out in twelve months with an update.

Thank you.

You

There you go: you just bought yourself a year of silence.

LET'S WRAP THIS UP WITH SOME IFS AND THENS.

IF YOU . . .	THEN TRY . . .
Think you need more experience before you start	Understanding that the most relevant experience will be to begin, and then continue
Believe failure is embarrassing	Reframing failure as an opportunity to learn, get up, and keep going
Desire to be honored for your past expertise and accomplishments	Recognizing that your past experience and accomplishments are part of the raw material you bring to your startup
Hear a voice that says you are not good enough	Talking to this voice and telling it: "I'm just getting started. Check back in a year and I'll show you how much of enough I really am."

Let's close with this letter from Rainier Maria Rilke.

Be patient toward all that is unsolved in your heart
and try to love the questions themselves . . .
like books that are written in a foreign language.
Do not seek the answers,
which cannot be given to you
because you would not be able to live them.
And the point is to live everything.
Live the questions now . . .

Resolve to be always beginning—
to be a beginner.

JUST BEGIN.

Do not wait for anything else to happen, inside or outside of you. The time to begin is now. Trust that your startup will show you the way.

GUIDED MEDITATION:
THE FIRST TIME

——

Take a deep breath. Bring back into your body all the energy that may be occupied in activities that are outside your body. One more breath, and once you feel centered and fully in this present moment, begin reading this:

Recall the time you first learned to ride a bike. You were probably six or seven years old. A parent or loving adult gifted you this bike, and you felt excited about the possibility of riding away, feeling the breeze on your cheeks. You fantasized about all of the places you could go, if you only knew how to ride it. You were a beginner. You were new to the task, but excited about it. You were humble—no pretenses. You knew you needed the help of others to get going, so there was likely an adult or older sibling behind you, holding the seat and prepared to begin a brisk and unpredictable jog, once you figured out that you could indeed balance yourself on the two-wheeled vehicle and take off.

Feel that energy of the beginner (visualize and pause after each of these):

- The excitement
- The acceptance of temporary failure on the road to success
- The gratitude for those who hold the seat so we won't fall

- The patience to get up time after time
- The reward of this beginner mindset

Take a few more breaths as you internalize this beginner's mindset, and begin to think of an area in your life that can benefit from this mindset. Perhaps this is your startup, job, relationship, sport, hobby, or your mindfulness practice. Can you afford not to be a beginner? What could move forward for you in your passion or endeavor if you approached it as a beginner?

A closing deep breath.

TL;DR
(TOO LONG; DIDN'T READ)

- Being a beginner can be your special advantage, instead of a drawback.
- A beginner understands that temporary failure is part of enduring success.
- A beginner is free of expectations. Experts suffer from so much pressure to live up to expectations from themselves and others. But beginners—we are free! We are free to create and fail, and try again, and have a detour, and then succeed.
- Respond to the inner critic with a reminder that you are learning, the way you would shut down a bully.
- Even if you are experienced in your industry, consider looking at what you are doing through fresh eyes to see a different perspective.
- Don't delay. Don't wait to acquire any type of additional skill or insight. Begin now.

CHAPTER 2

SINGLE DEEP FOCUS

To enjoy good health,
to bring true happiness to one's family,
to bring peace to all,
one must first discipline and control
one's own mind.
—Bukkyō Dendō Kyōkai

TALE FROM THE TRENCHES

Two weeks after embarking on my startup adventure, I posted on LinkedIn, announcing that I had started Seeker Health to help biotech companies find patients for clinical trials in rare diseases. "Nothing happens without patients," I said, "and we will work to find them."

A colleague, John, saw my post and reached out. He shared that he had just taken a role at a biotech company that was developing a treatment for solid tumors for patients with very rare gene mutations. The company had developed an educational website about the clinical trial and was in need of more targeted traffic. This trial was the main priority for this emerging biotech with publicly traded stock, and he wanted to try new approaches, such as social media advertising.

I was jumping with glee before the call even ended. I told him I would prepare a proposal and fly down to San Diego to share it in person. In a period of single deep focus, I created a proposal to describe the work, including mock ads, a list of measures we would track to determine success, a timeline, and budget.

Upon arriving in San Diego, I presented, as the only woman in the room, to a group of executives in a boardroom. I imagined this looked quite similar to presenting to venture capitalists, except that the group in front of me was willing to pay for a service, without asking for any equity in return.

The execs had interesting and important questions: What about approvals? How would I integrate the campaign with their current website? How long to see results in the shape of registration forms filled out by patients? Did I have any suggestions for their current registration form? I fielded their questions with delight because they were rounding out the profile of my customer with their main concerns. Next time around, all of these answers would already be spelled out in my presentation.

A few days later, I signed my first customer, who, get this . . . wanted a nine-month contract! Time to celebrate that a) I had found myself a salary of sorts, and b) I had nine months to learn more about how to help them solve more problems, and grow Seeker Health.

I began working on creating the campaign. For clinical trials, all patient-facing materials need to be approved by an institutional review board (IRB), and I provided the customer with a packet for submission, knowing it would take a few weeks to hear back.

The following Thursday, my mom flew from New York to visit me, so we could attend a weekend workshop at one of my favorite retreat centers in the world, the Esalen Institute. This was a special visit: since my father had passed away in July, this workshop was meant to ease my mother's pain as a newfound widow. A few years back, I found out I could come to Esalen in pain, but when faced with that magnificent cliff perching above the Pacific Ocean in Big Sur, I would find peace and clarity. In life, we come to ends that feel like stiff cliffs that drop you fast and hard, but at the bottom of that drop there's an ocean of peace to wash away what no longer serves the present moment. In her moment of pain over the loss of my father, I wanted my mother to experience this.

At Esalen, Wi-Fi is limited to non-mealtimes. Because I was expecting an answer from my new (and only) customer, I connected my phone to the internet to check email. A part of me wished I hadn't. The news wasn't good.

The IRB had rejected my submission.

Excellent. I had a grieving mother, one single client, a rejected submission, and no cell service.

"Write John back," my mom said. "I'll go to the workshop and meet you after."

I wrote back to ask for more information and devise a plan. John replied quickly that the IRB had rejected because we hadn't provided information on how we would control the social media campaign and monitor or prevent user-generated content.

That was sufficient direction for me to enter one of the most productive spells of single deep focus I have ever had in my life. The room went away, the people went away, the ocean went away. It was just me and the laptop.

I opened a Word doc and titled it "Social Media Control Procedure." I used the limited internet to research settings options on the Facebook page and ads to eliminate or minimize user-generated content. I typed, edited, typed more ferociously, and edited again.

My mom came back from the evening workshop, and said, "Sandra, don't worry if you have to work. I know how it goes." True, she worked as a financial advisor her entire adult life and served as a superb working-mom role model to me.

"Mom," I said, "I think I figured it out, and I sent the customer a possible solution."

Before I could read John's next email, which said, "I think this will do the trick. Thanks for pulling this together so quickly," I heard my mom say: "I always knew you would figure it out." I spent the next two days in Esalen mode: mindful, aware, conscious, grateful, and not checking email.

The IRB approved the campaign, and that Social Media Control Procedure, developed during one burst of single deep focus, is still used today in all of our submissions. This customer remained with Seeker Health for over two years. And my mom let the Pacific Ocean wash away some of her pain over the loss of my father.

THE TEACHING: CULTIVATE SINGLE DEEP FOCUS

What you are creating depends on your attention, like you depend on air. This devoted attention is a basic ingredient for creating something of value, such as a company, a book, or any other creative work that you may feel called upon to produce. I call this single deep focus.

Single deep focus is the ability to focus without distraction on a single task that is critical to your venture. During this time, you allow your brain, body, and soul to contribute all it has to offer into this one single task.

Author Cal Newport refers to this state as "deep work." Other experts refer to this type of attention as a gateway to "flow," that sought-after state in which people typically experience deep enjoyment, creativity, and total involvement with the task at hand and life itself.

I'll define this mental state in even more extreme terms: should the object that you most desire in life (your childhood celebrity crush, a bag with $100 million) happen to appear in your peripheral vision during a period of single deep focus, you wouldn't even *see* it. That type of focus is what I'd like you to harness as you are working on building the vital organs for your business.

This type of devoted attention to the important tasks for creating or building a new venture brings the following benefits:

- Allows you to prioritize what's important for your startup
- Clarifies what in your life deserves your single, deep focus
- Creates a shield, a boundary of protection, from distractions
- Builds intimacy with your startup. In that moment of single deep focus, your startup is getting all of you.

Critical tasks in startup life that really benefit from one or more periods of single deep focus include:

- Creating a pitch deck—the set of slides that explains and sells your business to customers, partners, or investors
- Designing a product or service
- Programming software
- Defining key features of your service or product
- Reviewing user testing data
- Reviewing résumés for key hires
- Writing a user manual
- Writing a patent application
- Creating a sales presentation
- Researching customer needs and objections
- Researching customer leads and connections
- Requesting customer feedback
- Creating a proposal template
- Creating a proposal for a potential customer
- Populating a due diligence data room for an acquisition deal
- **In other words, the really important stuff you'll do to move your startup forward**

The opposite of single deep focus is distraction. We've all experienced distraction, though we may not always admit to ourselves that we are indeed totally and utterly distracted. Here are some examples that may resonate:

- Distraction looks like the employee who decided to work on a pitch deck, while listening to a telecon on the new client billing procedure, while checking email at five-minute intervals. Is this employee going to create an excellent pitch deck? No.

- Distraction looks like the spouses who agreed to spend time together connecting about their days and lives—but instead their noses are in their respective phones at the first beep. Are these spouses going to feel connected after this time together? No.

- Distraction looks like parents who come home early— only to be on their laptops working for another two hours, while their kids are hungry for food and attention. Are those children going to feel cared for during those two hours? No.

Sources of distraction are pesky, irreverent, and all-knowing. You may be more aware of external interruption sources such as devices, people, and noise, rather than internal sources such as hunger or fatigue, and the peskiest ones: lack of interest and self-doubt.

Some of our distraction is completely natural. In *Hyperfocus*, Chris Bailey notes that "our drive toward distractions is made worse by our brain's built-in novelty bias." In essence, we are wired to be attracted to new things and to shift our attention there, over and over again.

But your startup needs your focus, so let's begin to break down these distractions, because once you start naming the body parts of the monster, it starts to shrink in size. Just watch.

THE DISTRACTION MONSTER
AND ITS VENOMOUS WAYS

VENOM SOURCE 1:
Internal Interruptions Posed by Your Mind
ANTIDOTE:
Call it, then shift it. Repeat after me: the work has to get done.

- Fear: You are afraid to fail. You are afraid to succeed. You won't know what will happen until you get the work done.
- Lack of interest: I hear you. You didn't start your own company to work on slides every day, and you hate PowerPoint and all slide-making software, and you should have a person who's in charge of this. OK, look around. Right—there's no one else to do this work, so you have to do the work.
- Self-doubt: You don't know if you can do this task, or any of it. Why didn't you just stay in corporate with the steady paycheck and the all-day meetings? Right. Because you wanted to create something impactful, valuable, and special.
- Perfectionism: Why even start, if what you finish won't be perfect? Your competitors aren't perfect either. Some don't even send out the proposals they promised they would. Reid Hoffman, founder of LinkedIn, says, "If you are not embarrassed by the first version of your product, you've launched too late." So, get the "imperfect" work done.

VENOM SOURCE 2:
External Interruptions
ANTIDOTE:
Turn them all off.

- Email: Turn it off. If need be, use an out-of-office notification saying you will be checking email next at, let's say, three p.m. Provide an alternate contact for your sender to reach out to.
- Messaging devices, social platforms, and vibrating watches: Turn them all off.
- Loud environment: Choose a quiet place that supports your work, such as a library or private office.
- People who need something: Turn them off. Let them know you are working on something important and you will be occupied for a few hours.
- Wi-Fi: Turn it off. "I need to google that"—try to avoid this at all costs during your creation stage. If your project absolutely needs outside research, then conquer this possible distraction by writing down what you'll search for on a Post-it note and put it as close to the middle of your screen as possible. This way, when you end up looking at puppies dressed like unicorns, you'll have a way to bring yourself back in focus.

VENOM SOURCE 3:
Internal Interruptions of the Bodily Kind
ANTIDOTE:
Feed, water, and empty.

- Hunger: Eat a light meal before you start your period of single deep focus.
- Thirst: Secure a beverage for yourself, but don't start drinking until you've worked for a bit.
- Bathroom: Absolutely go to the bathroom before you begin your period of single deep focus.

THE DISTRACTION MONSTER
AND HOW TO TAME IT

CALL & SHIFT THESE	TURN THESE OFF	PREEMPT THESE
<ul><li>I'm afraid.</li><li>I'm not interested.</li><li>I don't think I can do it.</li><li>If it's not perfect, I'd rather not do it.</li></ul>	<ul><li>Email</li><li>Messaging platforms</li><li>Vibrating watches</li><li>Loud environments</li><li>Needy people</li><li>Wi-Fi</li><li>Google</li></ul>	<ul><li>Hunger</li><li>Thirst</li><li>Bathroom</li></ul>

Now that you have the tools to conquer the Distraction Monster, let's work on cultivating a practice of single deep focus.

A PRACTICE OF SINGLE DEEP FOCUS

CREATE A CONTAINER

The container you create should be a ritual or routine. You are in charge of creating the container that promotes deep focus. As you plan and design your single deep focus cocoon, do not overlook the interruptions described above. Take care to eliminate any and all types of interruptions. Turn off your phone ringer; close messaging apps, email, and your web browser. Go to the bathroom, come back and close the door, and begin.

SET YOUR INTENTION . . . ONE INTENTION

When you set your intention, you clarify to your mind what you are doing during your period of single deep focus and why. *Plant Seed, Pull Weed*, a delight of a mindfulness book by Geri Larkin, states: "It is pretty amazing when you think about it—how our lives are transformed act by act." Each one of these acts requires intention and then focus. As an example, you may say to yourself: "Today, I'll give two hours of single deep focus to my sales slide deck, because it's a critical tool for us to win more business." You can take a piece of paper and write:

Sales Slide Deck
2 Hours
Win More Business

By then, you have controlled your environment and can now set to focus on what you're working on, while knowing why this is deserving of your precious time.

You'll learn more in chapter 3 about determining the actions that can make the most impact on your business.

SET A TIME LIMIT

Your attention span is not limitless. You are not a robot who can work indefinitely without rest or refuel. Single deep focus is meant to be a temporary state, engineered by you to maximize creativity, quality, and productivity.

After the time limit has elapsed, the period of single deep focus is officially over. Most times, you'll be ready to get up, move around, and allow your eyes and mind to focus on something else.

Sometimes, you may get so involved that you want to continue. I advise you to really check in with yourself by asking: "Can I continue to produce high-level work at this time, or am

I better off picking this up again when my body and brain have had some rest?"

Listen closely for the answer. Working when you are tired can be counterproductive and result in undoing the incredible progress you have made.

PRACTICE EVERY (WORK)DAY

Each day, choose one area that will obtain your single deep focus for a period of time. Write it down on a piece of paper to create a mini contract with yourself to give this area your full attention for a period of time. The area of deep focus may change from day to day, but the mind muscles exercised in that period of focus are the same. Note that inspiration is not a prerequisite for creation, but time is. You need not be inspired at the moment of creation. Instead, you need to allocate time to create, and once you begin, the magic happens. You can't predict what will emerge, and thus all you can do is carve out the time to create. Daily practice will make these muscles toned, strong, and beautifully productive. And before long, you'll wake up to a venture that's no longer starting; it's building.

GUIDED MEDITATION:
SINGLE DEEP FOCUS

Close your eyes. Take a deep breath. Bring back into your body all the energy that may be occupied in activities that are outside of your body.

One more breath; hold it for four seconds. As you breathe out, release any and all remaining distractions. Here you are, simply present in this moment.

In this state of relaxation, I'd like you to do a bit of mental scavenging and search for an area that needs your attention. Perhaps this is a new feature for your software, a new scene for your book, a new type of customer you'd like to attract, or a piece of art in your mind that doesn't yet exist in the physical realm.

Ponder these questions:

- What would transform for you if you decide to approach this area with single deep focus?
- What would happen if today, or tomorrow, you spent one to two hours in single deep focus for creativity and production in this area?
- Can you commit today to one session of single deep focus to investigate what manifests from it? I certainly hope you can, and I support you in that commitment.

One more deep focused breath to seal in this intention of SINGLE DEEP FOCUS for days and weeks to come. Open your eyes. Go get it.

TL;DR

———

- Your creation depends on your attention like you depend on air.

- **Set a Single Intention:** Setting a "theme" for your deep work moment will help you stay strong against distractions of other urgent but less important tasks.

- **Create a Container:** Whatever space you associate with your best focus and productivity, turn it into a cocoon of quiet that you can retreat to regularly without disturbance.

- **Set a Time Limit:** If you don't take an intentional break, your body and brain will take one for you, by finding ways to wander off or space out. Setting a time limit will also empower you to respect a healthy work/life balance.

- **Practice Every Day:** Cultivating the ability to focus requires practice. The more you do, the more you can do.

PART 2

BUILD

CHAPTER 3

THE FLOW IS FORWARD

As you start to walk on the way, the way appears.
—Rumi

TALE FROM THE TRENCHES

My feet were aching. My hair was drenched in sweat. My iPod was out of songs. My family was waiting with a Uruguayan flag at mile 21 in Manhattan, but I had just hit the very real wall at mile 20 in the Bronx. I had decided to run the 2004 New York City Marathon because I needed an athletic redemption, after some very nonathletic formative years. My goal was purely to finish—however long it took. Now, with twenty miles behind me, and six more interminable miles to go, I felt ready to quit. I shuffled some more when two thoughts struck me like lightning.

First, I had come too far to quit now. The only reason to quit now was a heart attack. Second, I realized all I had to do was keep moving forward. That's it. One foot forward, the other foot forward. One, then the other. I'd like to say I flowed forward toward the finish line, but we all know I shuffled. By the time I finished the 26.2 miles, the sun had set and the finish tent was empty except for a few dozen fellow shufflers, but I was happy and transformed. I'd broken through the wall, I'd covered the distance . . . one step at a time, and the flow was forward.

Startup work is a lot like a marathon. "Overnight success" is actually the result of years of hard work. The key is to find ways to keep moving forward no matter what, even if it is at the pace of a turtle. For Seeker Health, this forward flow manifested in the growing needs of our customers for more, more, more.

In mid 2016, with five customers on board, I learned that customers not only needed a social media campaign, but they also needed a trial website, a data collection form, and most important, a secure system to manage all of the referrals we were generating. Customer number five in particular, a former Nora colleague, was specifically asking for this capability expansion, and willing to give us a try as we built all of these.

The flow is forward, and so I started using as many off-the-shelf tools as possible to keep meeting customer demand, until we came to the final need, for a patient lead management system. This component needed to be built from scratch and was going to require programmers, money, time, and quality testing, and user manuals, and user training and hosting, and, and, and—deep breath . . . beginner's mindset.

A friend close to the business said: "Don't build a product within a service business. It doesn't usually work out." I responded with complete conviction: "I have to."

Specifically, I had to build software in order to:

- Deliver an end-to-end customer experience and avoid the use of multiple vendors
- Automate as much of the process as possible, and scale by letting the "machine" do most of the work

- Differentiate against competitors, both alive and those yet to be born
- Move the business forward. This was the next logical thing to grow the business and its impact. A business that isn't moving forward is moving backward.

There was only one problem—actually two: I'm not a programmer, and I've never developed software. I called on an industry consultant to help me write down what I wanted the software to do, apparently called the "feature set," and, capture the user interface requirements to manifest those features, known as "wireframes," and build a request for proposal (RFP).

I received three responses to the RFP, chose the local over the offshore developers, and set a project timeline. The cost of development was about $150,000 for the first version, plus $3,000 per month for maintenance. (In chapter 4, I'll address why I didn't raise outside funding to pay for software development.)

I project-managed the software contractors like a hawk. Right, I might not have known how to code, but I knew how to manage a project to a timeline. Which features are next? Which user types are complete? What's left to do to give it a test run?

In early 2017, we launched version 1.0 of the Seeker Portal, a secure patient lead management system. Nine months later, we launched version 2.0 with a major user interface upgrade. The Seeker Portal expanded what we could do for customers, increased the value of our contracts, and empowered the company to scale to an unlimited number of customers.

A startup is a marathon, with a number of sprints, more than a few hurdles to overcome, and the flow is forward. So I kept going.

THE TEACHING: THE BEST NEXT ACTION TO TAKE TODAY

What you are creating benefits from forward motion—that is, chopping the wood every single day. The entire point of a startup is to continue to grow until reaching a point of maturity. As the leader of your startup, your job is to facilitate this growth—and chop wood each day.

To do so, each morning, ask yourself this:

BASIC DAILY QUESTION:
WHAT IS THE BEST NEXT ACTION I CAN TAKE TODAY?

You know your startup best, and usually there are so many things to do that the list is too long and overwhelming. What you are looking for instead is not a massive, repulsive to-do list, but instead the best action to take right now, today.

If the answer isn't coming to you easily today, no worries. Consider this list of prompts to get the wheels turning:

- How can my startup increase current customer satisfaction?
- How can my startup increase the closing rate for potential customers in the pipeline?
- How can my startup attract new potential customers?
- What new features/services are needed to continue to grow?
- How can my startup attract new hires?

- How can I contain or reduce costs?
- How can I increase brand awareness with my target customers?

Because attention wanders, it helps to write down what you want to accomplish today, this week, this month, this quarter, and this year. At a minimum, writing your daily goals in a notebook or directly on your online calendar can work wonders to keep you focused on what's the best next action to take. If you'd like to level up, consider the "bullet journal method," a cross-functional technique for taking notes, downloading ideas, and organizing present and future work.

I've adapted the bullet journal method as follows:

- I begin a notebook by numbering pages.
- I create an index.
- I list the goals for that year.
- I create a grid to contain twelve months, and I list goals and events for each month.
- I create monthly trackers for each month, but only two to three months at a time, and I leave enough room in each month for note-taking.
- On the left-hand side of the journal spread, I list the days and annotate any important events, deadlines, and travel.
- On the right-hand side of the journal spread, I divide the page horizontally into thirds. I label each "work," "family," "personal." In each rectangle I write down the goals for that month for each category.
- I leave my notebook open to this spread, or I insert the marker here to enable quickly locating what I'm working toward.

In terms of how to advance your startup, I'd like to empower you as the source of the best answer for your startup. It's fine to seek advice from mentors, experts, and teachers, but remember that none of them created the thing. *You* created the thing.

Whatever you do, remember that the flow is forward. Chop the wood every day, and keep moving forward.

GUIDED MEDITATION:
FINDING YOUR NEXT BEST STEP

For this meditation, you may want to have a piece of paper to journal the insights you gain.

Close your eyes. Take a deep breath. Bring back into your body all the energy that may be occupied in activities that are outside of your body. One more breath; hold it for four seconds, and as you breathe out, release any and all remaining distractions. Here you are, simply present in this moment.

In this state of mindful focus, begin to build some distance between you and your startup. As founders, our startups tend to live inside of ourselves. With this exercise, I would like to build some distance from it now. Across the room, picture a table—large and sturdy enough to hold your startup for this period of meditation.

Once you can see the table, place your startup on it. All of it.

The startup is now on the table, which means it's no longer inside of you, and you have distance.

Now, take a deep breath, and in your mind only, without moving a muscle, begin to walk around the table and observe your startup from a distance.

What have you built so far? What problems is it solving? What is its current impact on the market, on humanity, and on you? See what you've built.

Whatever this is, it didn't exist before you created it. Marvel at that.

Another deep breath to achieve maximum relaxation and space from your startup. Now ask yourself the critical question:

What is the best next action I can take?

* Sense for images, words, and sounds.
* Jot them down.
* Ask the question again.

What is the best next action I can take?

* Sense for intuition and feelings.
* Jot them down.

One more deep breath to seal in your awareness of the next step and how you'll flow forward in the days and weeks to come.

Open your eyes. And go get it.

TL;DR

____

- The flow of progress is forward. Keep the momentum going, no matter what.
- While momentum must be forward, it need not be fast. Sometimes you'll need to sprint, and sometimes a shuffle will do.
- Ask yourself each day: **What is the best next action I can take today?**
- Let the voice and needs of your customers be your guide. Their stake in your success is the most objective.
- Seek and absorb advice from others, but always trust yourself to make the final decision, even if it is counterintuitive to mainstream beliefs.
- Because our startup is a creation close to us, sometimes things can get personal. Use mindfulness and meditation to observe your project from a distance and gain objective clarity on the best next steps.

CHAPTER 4

DEEP POCKETS ARE NEVER DEEP ENOUGH

Those deep pockets . . . they'll
never be deep enough
to buy all the passion, ingenuity,
and determination
it takes to have success over the long haul.
—Daymond John, *The Power of Broke*

TALE FROM THE TRENCHES

As I plunged into software development, this was the moment when perhaps I could have considered raising investor funding. So why did I take what appears to be the path less traveled for startups in technology? At least ten reasons, and probably more.

1. **I didn't need investor money.** Because I had started Seeker Health by providing digital media campaigns and had five paying customers, I was not only

collecting significant revenue but making a profit, which allowed me to pay for software development.

2. **I wasn't in the mood to hear "no."** Seeker Health was growing, and I was flowing forward where the market was showing me opportunities. Pitching venture capitalists as a first-time founder would have likely entailed hearing fifty "nos" to get one "yes." I decided my time would be better spent pitching potential customers, where my odds of hearing a "yes" were proving closer to 70 percent.

3. **I saw continued customer demand.** More and more customers, now well beyond my immediate network, were reaching out to learn about Seeker Health. This demand was further supported by industry fundamentals: 80 percent of emerging biotech companies were developing treatments in rare disease or oncology, our areas of focus. If only a portion of these came to Seeker Health for clinical trial enrollment, we would be just fine.

4. **I didn't want to give away equity.** I was growing my third baby, and giving away 20 percent of its body (that's like an arm *and* a leg, or all the internal organs!) seemed grotesque to me. Also, along the way, a colleague running a much larger business said, "You can own 10 percent of a $100 million company with a complicated capitalization table and control structure, or you can own 100 percent of a $10 million company and have a simpler life." This resonated for me, especially for my first startup, and I was going to own all of it for as long as I could.

5. **I didn't want investor returns to become the central focus of the business.** Taking on funding from investors promotes investor returns as a top goal for the company. Venture capitalist firms work for their limited partners, who entrust large sums of money for the possibility of an outsized return. I worked in healthcare for fifteen years because I wanted to spend my life working on products that made a difference in people's lives. I wanted to stick to that central focus.

6. **I didn't want the low probability and high pressure of an outlier investor return.** VCs are looking for the 1 percent of startups that will reach unicorn status and deliver an outsized return for their funds. While I love ambitious goals, my ambitious goal was to build a company that accelerated patient finding in a profitable way, so that the company can sustain its employees, founder, and itself.

7. **I didn't want to sort through advice that might not be relevant to my business.** While I recognize that many venture capital firms provide valuable connections and business-building advice to founders, for my particular startup, the best advice would come from those we served directly, our customers and patients, who demanded no equity in return.

8. **I could not fathom a celebration for taking other people's money.** Tech media writes about fundraising milestones like they're the celebration of the century. Meanwhile, when a company raises funding, what just happened is that the founders gave a large chunk of equity in exchange for other people's money to work toward the far-fetched probability of an outsized

return for investors. This use of other people's money is most celebrated in startup culture. You know who should be celebrated instead? People who build profitable, self-sustaining companies.

9. **I believe financial responsibility is a basis for success.** Startups that are flush with cash drown in it. They buy a bunch of Ping-Pong tables they don't need, and overstaff with too-expensive talent they will then overfeed. I saw this in corporate America too, where rich companies waste resources, just because they can. But I grew up with the opposite in my family of origin, where we would go to the supermarket with $40 and buy $100 worth of food by maximizing coupons and deals. Humans spend more responsibly when the money is theirs (not borrowed) and when the supply of money is scarce.

10. **Fundraising exhausts founders, leaving less energy to build.** If the founder's first priority is fundraising, then you can guess where product and customers sit. Not at the top. I've seen many founders in my network end up exhausted after raising a round of funding, needing to recover from the raise before they can even begin to focus on the real deal: the product and customers.

It turns out that when it comes to funding, I'm less alone than I felt. Sources show that:[4]

---

4. Meredith Wood, "Raising Capital for Startups: 8 Statistics That Will Surprise You," fundera (website), February 3, 2020, https://www.fundera.com/resources/startup-funding-statistics.

- Only 0.05 percent of startups raise venture capital.
- Of startups that raised seed rounds, 1 percent reached unicorn status of >$1 billion valuation.

Please don't get me wrong: if my startup had had to raise venture funding, I would have certainly engaged with unicorn hunters to make that funding appear. And I recognize that there may have been some benefits to those interactions. Instead, I chose to focus on manifesting traction for my startup. This time around, that traction proved to be enough to support the investments I had to make in the business.

THE TEACHING: THE POWER
OF PAYING CUSTOMERS

Paying customers should be your central focus for more reasons than just funding. Early-paying customers may be able to support the continuous development of your product and service. More important, early-paying customers allow you to learn how to maximize the value that you can provide to them. You begin by selling them A, and in that process recognize that they need B and C too, and you begin to build in that direction.

Here are the superpowers of early-paying customers:

SUPERPOWER	EARLY-PAYING CUSTOMERS ARE AWESOME BECAUSE . . .
Accelerated Product Development	They are willing to buy a minimally viable product, and you can use this opportunity to gain insights on other needs they may have, accelerating product development.
Informed Market Development	They provide data on their problem and need, so you can continue to adjust your market fit to the segment most likely to adopt your full solutions. Some of these early-paying customers may not be able to be retained as the company builds in a specific direction, and that's OK.
No Equity Required	They do not require you to issue equity. Instead, they want their problem solved, and they are willing to pay for it.
Referral to Additional Customers	They may refer other customers just like them or better.

I can see what you're thinking—you're planning to raise funds anyway, so who needs early-paying customers. Well, if you end up raising venture capital in exchange for equity, then having paying customers will only help your case. In fact, even incubators and angel investors, who are willing to pony up money for the earliest stages of a company's operation, are looking to invest in companies with some evidence of traction. The following are the requirements for a sample incubator:

- **For enterprise or marketplace startups:** $5,000 to $100,000 per month in gross profit with at least 20 percent growth, month on month
- **For consumer products:** 5,000 daily active users with at least 5 percent week-on-week growth

There's no way around it: a brilliant idea is not a business. A business is an organization offering a product or service that a set of customers is willing to use and/or pay for. Acquiring these early users or paying customers requires passion, ingenuity, and determination, and this becomes a powerful engine for growing your startup—with or without venture funding.

GUIDED MEDITATION:
PASSION, INGENUITY, AND DETERMINATION

Take a deep breath in and close your eyes.

For a moment, I'd like you to maneuver your mind to eliminate all providers of funding for equity. What I'm looking for is for you to enter into a mindset in which angel investors, seed rounds, Series A, and Series B do not exist. Don't worry, they'll still be there when you're done with this meditation.

Now, begin walking around this world without VC, and find a place in your mind to sit down for a moment and contemplate the following questions:

Since there's no VC in this mind world, no possibility for someone to give you funds for a chunk of your company, then you are faced with finding another option to build your business.

What options exist for you? How do you deliver, as soon as possible, something that customers would be willing to pay for? What other sources of funds might exist in your life?

Is there an asset that might be able to be sold?

Is there a loan that might be possible?

Is there a way to monetize your passion into the funds required for your business?

Spend another few seconds collecting the harvest from this meditation.

Open your eyes. And feel free to pursue the sources of funding available to you.

TL;DR

- Interrogate your need for venture capital, knowing that many startups neither need this type of funding, nor are they a good fit for it.
- Consider alternative funding sources before deciding to give away a large chunk of equity.
- Apply passion, ingenuity, and determination to the process of finding the first few paying customers for your business.
- Work with these early-paying customers to ensure you are providing a full solve to their problem—that is, that you've found a secure product/market fit.

CHAPTER 5

FULL-ON TRANSFORMATION TO PAYING CUSTOMERS

Do you love your idea?
Does it feel right on instinct?
Are you willing to bleed for it?
—Steven Pressfield, *Do the Work*

TALE FROM THE TRENCHES

The needle punctured my vein. My body stiffened. "Almost done," he lied. Blood, my blood began to flow into the first of three vials. The vials bore my name and the name of the clinical trial I was participating in—joined together by blood. I was literally bleeding for my startup, and happy to do it.

Prior to starting Seeker Health, I had been involved in several clinical trials for rare-disease populations eagerly expecting the first treatment for their condition. I was involved in assessing feasibility, creating strategies to enroll participants, and developing timelines to accelerate filing with regulatory agencies. Since starting Seeker Health, I had been involved in dozens of clinical trials, reviewing inclusion and exclusion criteria, and setting up our platform to find the desired patient population. But I had never been a clinical trial participant myself.

I began scanning my body for conditions that might make me eligible for a clinical trial. I was born healthy and haven't acquired any serious conditions, but I do have a mild-to-moderate skin condition that occasionally bothers me. In the name of science, getting closer to my customer, and maybe finding a solution to my condition, I sought to find a clinical trial near me. As I was sitting down to breakfast on a Sunday morning, I saw an ad in the paper version of the *Palo Alto Weekly* for a clinical trial for my skin condition at a nearby university hospital. I clipped the ad and called the number the following Monday. A clinical coordinator began to ask me questions related to the entry criteria for the study. She went question by question, boring us both. Then she collected my contact information, and I had to spell my last name three times, and speak my email address!

The irony of this low-tech interaction, and the need for Seeker Health, was palpable: Instead of seeing the ad online as powered by Seeker Health, I clipped an ad from the free local paper and had to wait till Monday to begin the process. Instead of completing an online prescreener as powered by Seeker Health, a clinical coordinator asked me questions by phone and asked me to spell my last name three times, all of which took ten times longer than an online prescreening form. Instead of receiving an immediate communication letting me know the contact information of the clinical coordinator, I had to ask her for her phone number, and was never able to obtain her email.

I enrolled in the clinical trial, open and willing to learn more about how Seeker Health could best serve patients, clinics, and drug developers. For the pre-dosing blood draw, the coordinator accompanied me to the lab and helped me skip the line of people waiting.

"You sure?" I asked. I really value fairness, and that seemed unfair.

"Definitely. You are in a clinical trial, volunteering your body and data."

She had a point, but these special privileges didn't last long, and I found myself waiting an average of half an hour for the remaining visits, all of which required three vials of my fresh blood.

The three monthly vials of my blood were well worth validating the problems our team was trying to solve at Seeker Health. During the time I participated in the clinical trial, I picked up another half-dozen ideas to reduce the burden on patients, sites, and biopharmaceutical companies.

While the side effects of the investigational medicine or placebo I received were not bad at all, and I didn't even grow an eleventh finger, what grew instead were my insights into the workings, burdens, and needs of the stakeholders in a clinical trial. These would not have been available to me as just a professional working in the field.

What's more, bleeding for my startup helped me realize that the ultimate need—of our patients, our customers, our employees—is for transformation. Patients need a medicine that will transform an unbearable condition into a bearable one. Biopharmaceutical companies want to fully enroll their clinical trials, to transform into a company with an (or another) approved treatment. Our employees want careers that transform a mere job into a calling, a mission, a passion. Transformation was the goal for all of these stakeholders, and my startup was the vehicle.

THE TEACHING: SERVE YOUR FELLOW NEEDY HUMANS FOR IMPACTFUL TRANSFORMATION

Your startup will have the most value once you can connect your work to serving a true human need. You are in luck, because humans are extremely needy.

Exhibit A: Humans Are Extremely Needy[5]
The Heart-Canvas uses the graphical metaphor of a flower to represent life and the many needs of human beings. You are needy. So am I. So is every human being (and animals and plants, too). The flowerpot represents all the survival needs, like air, water, shelter, food, and movement. Each petal represents the eight broad categories of needs: community, sustainability, autonomy, honesty, well-being, meaning, peace, empathy. Above all of these needs is the highest need, for transcendence. I love this tool because it depicts the universal needs of humans by category. The great news is that most of these needs translate into potential business opportunities to serve human beings!

Take the petal of community, for example. Many of the successful businesses of the last decade have formed to address needs in this area.

---

5. Heart-Canvas is the sole copyright of Compassionate Connecting and included here with permission. Developed by James Prieto and available at www. Heart-Canvas.com. The needs flower was inspired by Jim and Jori Manske's needs wheel (RadicalCompassion.com) and modified to match the natural metaphor of a flower—giving full representation to personal, interpersonal, physical, and transcendent needs.

Facebook—to fill the need for connection to your family and friends and your ninth grade sweetheart.

Whatsapp—to fill the need for immediate, global communication.

Slack—to fill the need for collaboration among work teams.

Kickstarter—to fill the need for partnership for projects.

Your startup is much more likely to succeed if:

1. **You understand the needs of your customers.** This involves truly putting yourself in the shoes of your customers. If it takes three monthly vials of fresh blood to find out, so be it.

   - What's your customers' current problem(s)?
   - What are their pain points?
   - What's their current experience?
   - What solutions do they desire?

2. **You fill customer needs as deeply and fully as possible.** This involves providing end-to-end solutions with a true benefit to your customer.

   - How does your solution fix the problem?
   - Does it create any new problems for your customers, which you should strive to solve too?

3. **You effectively target your solution to a profitable segment.** Most solutions require targeting. While Facebook now operates at mass scale with 2.4 billion users, out of the 7.7 billion humans alive on the planet, the company began in a very targeted way: on college campuses, choosing an opportune target segment of the population that would adopt the product

with fervor. (More on segmentation and positioning in chapter 6.)

When you connect your work to serving a deep need, product/market fit will come easily and automatically.

GUIDED MEDITATION:
CONNECTING TO YOUR ABILITY TO SERVE

Find a nice comfortable place to sit or lie down. Take a deep breath, and begin to relax your body. Sense a warm, comforting light at the crown of your head.

Let's travel into your heart. Take your shoes off very slowly, and with the greatest level of care, take a step into your heart.

Are you inside? Can you see how big your heart is? Take a few steps into your heart. What do you see? What are the images that pop into your mind? Walk around some more.

What's left to do with the remaining ticktocks of this big heart? What does it want to do? How does it want to serve?

Collect all of the details: the colors, the sounds, the people, the words, the objects.

- How does your heart want to serve?
- Who needs this service?
- What problems do they have?

Collect the imagery you summoned, and breathe it in. The time to serve is now. Deep breath in, and out.

TL;DR

———

- Find problems by walking in your customers' shoes.
- Seek to solve a problem before seeking to start a business.
- People are needy, which means business ideas and opportunities are abundant.
- Don't solve just any need. Make sure it is one that connects with you and fills your heart with a sense of purpose, as though you were chosen for it.
- A deep purpose for what you are doing will provide the staying power needed to endure.

CHAPTER 6

TALK TO YOUR COMPETITORS

*Never compare your insides to
someone else's outsides.*
—Unknown

TALE FROM THE TRENCHES

When I started Seeker Health, I knew there were a lot of advertising agencies attempting to craft campaigns to enroll patients in clinical trials, but I wasn't worried. Having been a client of many ad agencies, I had first-hand experience with how their work was generally slow and plagued with daily agonies over the hue of the sunset on the website. Clinical trials needed efficiency, speed, and a focus on results, so differentiating against marketing agencies was easy. I knew there were some trial recruitment companies, but they tended to shy away from rare diseases, chucking those patients as too hard to find.

I needed to learn more about my competitors, and it happened that Ben, a former colleague and friend who was a champion of Seeker Health and who was in a position to select vendors, took to sharing the names of other companies bidding for similar work. Ben would send me a quick email, such as "check out this new company in patient enrollment," and I would research and try to figure out if Seeker Health was different, and hopefully better.

A few months later, in February 2016, I came face to face with a gaggle of competitors at the Summit for Clinical Operations Executives. This almost mandatory, always crowded industry meeting was an excellent opportunity to discover more of Seeker Health's competitors and understand how to differentiate from them. In the exhibit halls, a handful of competitors staffed booths with coordinating backdrops and tablecloths, while in the sessions, additional companies presented their approaches to patient finding.

My mom always told me that you don't know the answer until you ask, and I'd like to show you how important it is to ask questions and take advantage of people's need to talk about themselves.

I approached a booth of what appeared to be a competitor of Seeker Health. The booth was staffed by men in matching shirts and beards. Easy targets. And I had the following conversation (*my thoughts are noted in italics*).

Me: Tell me a little about your company.
Beard: We find patients for clinical trials. (*Ha, so do we—not good.*)
Me: How do you do so?
Beard: We use digital advertising and bring patients into a system where they can be connected to sites. (*So, not good, too similar.*)
Me: What conditions do you work on?
Beard: Common conditions like acne, eczema, asthma, and the like. (*Excellent—Seeker Health can bring more value to rare and complex conditions.*)

He hands me his card. I hand him mine.

Me: Thanks. Do you do any work in rare diseases or oncology?

Beard: No, those are too hard to find. *(Good. Seeker Health can find them.)*

Me: How do you charge?

Beard: Well, sites buy a package from us to promote their study. *(Poor choice? Sites have lower budgets than sponsors.)*

He hands me a brochure that describes these packages.

Me: So, your customers are sites only?

Beard: Yes. *(This is great, I think. Our customers are bio-pharmaceutical companies, which are one level above the site, and commission our programs for multiple sites in one contract.)*

Take a moment to notice that like an interrogation, this conversation was one-directional. He's been put at the booth to talk about this company, and he's doing his job.

In the course of this industry meeting, researching Ben's weekly discovery of companies in patient recruitment, and additional interactions with clients and competitors, I learned there were still ways to differentiate Seeker Health, even in this crowded market.

First, I noticed that there were differences in the type of patients a company could specialize in finding, such as:

- Incidence of condition—common, specialty, rare, or ultrarare
- Type of condition—chronic or episodic
- Severity of condition—mild, moderate, or severe

Second, I saw there were varying types of potential customers that would be looking for patients to enroll, including:

- Emerging biopharma companies, which are generally startups in Phase 2 or 3 of clinical development, with a thirst for innovation and great urgency
- Midsize biopharma companies that are post-IPO, in Phase 3, and/or have an approved product, as well as more processes in place. They may still be able to act fast (sometimes)
- Large biopharma companies, such as a well-established company with multiple approved products, entrenched bureaucracy, and slow adoption of new technology
- Clinical research organizations (CROs), hired by biopharma sponsors to run the studies, and generally somewhat accountable for enrollment, though struggles in this area are common

Third, I saw that the differences in approach were many. There were companies mining electronic records, companies nurturing long-term databases, and companies hired by sites, versus sponsors.

Armed with this information, I crafted the following positioning statement for Seeker Health.

POSITIONING STATEMENT

For emerging biopharmaceutical companies and innovative CROs developing new life-saving treatments, Seeker Health is the most innovative end-to-end patient-finding platform that accelerates the finding of hard-to-find patients with complex conditions, in order to bring new treatments to those who need them as early as possible.

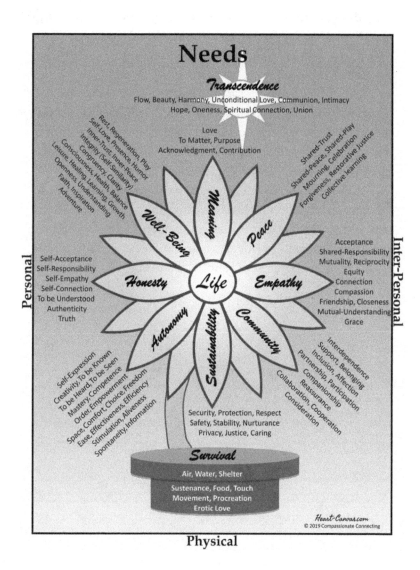

Physical

I didn't quite sit down to write this positioning statement on the first day of Seeker Health, because I didn't yet know enough to segment the market, but over time, I was able to produce this positioning statement and refine it.

Each time I learned of a new entrant in the market, I collected information to see if Seeker Health's differentiation was still valid. Especially in a crowded market, it was important to not be all things to all people, and to find the most valuable place where Seeker Health could serve and win.

As the years went by, Ben's emails about new competitors popping up left and right began to slow down. Were there fewer new entrants? Were companies going out of business? Yes, and yes. The winners were emerging, and at Seeker Health, we had found a differentiated spot from which to stay alive and grow.

THE TEACHING: THE IMPORTANCE OF POSITIONING

———

Competition is fundamental to business. The most attractive markets with a problem to solve will have multiple companies attempting to solve it. If you allow it and engage, your competitors will make your startup better by providing the exact information you need to position yourself at the highest value.

STEP 1: ANALYZE, STUDY, AND INTERROGATE COMPETITORS.
Face the fact that competition is the sunlight feeding the business jungle. Just like facing pain, facing your competition will cause its features to soften and its imperfections to magnify. You will discover that your competition is no smarter or harder working than you are. Your analysis and interrogation of the competition allows you to spot the differences and select the areas in which your startup can win.

Take a moment to think:
HOW CAN YOU BEGIN TO LEARN MORE ABOUT YOUR COMPETITORS?

STEP 2: SEGMENT YOUR MARKET.
To segment the market means to divide the market into smaller groups of customers who behave in similar ways or have similar needs.

Take a moment to think:
HOW WOULD YOU SEGMENT YOUR MARKET?

STEP 3: CHOOSE YOUR POSITIONING.
To position the company or product means to select the place
in which it intends to operate and the customer whose needs it
intends to deeply fulfill.

You may be asking: Why do I need to choose? Isn't my
startup better off making a product everyone wants to buy?
Well, let's look into this.

When you craft a position statement, you want to answer
these four questions:

1. **Who is your customer?**
   Question to ask: Who will buy your product or
   service?

2. **Why is your startup the most/best/only . . . ?**
   Questions to ask: What are you? How do you solve the
   problem?

3. **What key benefits does it provide?**
   Questions to ask: Why would a customer choose you
   versus your competitors? What is your special focus
   or superpower?

4. **How does it realize an ultimate benefit that is
   important, meaningful, and transcends you as a
   person?**
   Question to ask: Why are you spending your precious
   life doing this?

One final note on positioning: Your company needs positioning, and each of your products needs positioning. The
company's positioning is the umbrella under which properly
positioned products operate.

STEP 4: REFOCUS YOUR ATTENTION ON YOUR STARTUP.
Competition, while natural in business, is quite unnatural in mindfulness, which warns us about comparing ourselves to others. After you peek at your competitors, be sure to bring all of your attention back to your startup.

Your startup thrives on your ability to focus, not your ability to look over the fence.

GUIDED MEDITATION:
A PLACE IN THIS GARDEN

Take a deep breath and travel with me to a nearby garden in your mind. In this garden, you see a diversity of trees, plants, and flowers.

Look up at the sun. Now down at the plants. Notice which plants are touched by the sun. There's enough sun for all of them.

Now, look down at the earth. Then, back up at the trees, plants, and flowers around you. Notice how all of them draw nutrients from the ground. There are enough nutrients in the ground to feed all of them.

Sit in the garden. Could it be possible that your competitors are just like other trees, plants, or flowers in this garden? Could it be that there's enough sun, water, and nutrients for all?

Now, lie down in this garden. Do you think that the blue flower thinks hard about whether the tree over there is taking all of its sun? The blue flower thinks about being a blue flower. It thinks about the fact that there's a place in this garden for it. It feels at peace with the fact that it isn't alone in this garden but is a part of the garden. The blue flower's only job is to maximize its life.

It's the same for you and your startup. Can you see how there's enough sun, water, and nutrients for your startup, despite who else is in this market?

Your only job is to optimize the value and impact of your startup. Be like the blue flower and carry on, with the only thing that matters: maximizing the life of your own startup.

TL;DR

- Explore your competition to design your positioning in the market.
- Don't try to please all of the people. Be specific in the problem you solve and whom you solve it for.
- Craft a positioning statement that specifically addresses your customer, the problem you solve, benefits you provide, and your company's purpose for existing. Continue to assess that statement as the market provides you with further insight.
- Adopt an abundance mentality. In the business jungle, there is enough soil and sunlight to grow and nurture most species in the market.
- After you peek at your competitors, bring all of your attention back to optimizing the value and impact of your own startup.

CHAPTER 7

AT FIRST, HIRE CAPABLE BLANK SLATES

*Michelangelo is often quoted as having said
that inside every block of stone or marble
dwells a beautiful statue;
one need only remove the excess material
to reveal the work of art within.*
—Rosamund Stone Zander and
Benjamin Zander, *The Art of Possibility*

*I've come to believe that learning is
the essential unit of progress for startups.*
—Eric Ries, *The Lean Startup*

TALE FROM THE TRENCHES

"She hasn't worked for the last six years," my friend Caroline told me. She was cautious as she spoke, as if afraid to lose my interest with any part of her phrasing.

"She stopped working to raise her twins," Caroline continued. "And, Sandra, I met Sharon in person, and she's great. I have a good feeling about her for Seeker Health. Can I put you in touch?"

Many founders would say: "Caroline, thank you very much. I'll look into it," then file the résumé in the "Other" folder and forget the interaction ever took place. After all, many startups hire in the same way that established corporate America does: those educated at selective colleges, who've accumulated relevant and continuous work experience, who are generally very preoccupied with their outward accomplishments and reputation, and who can work all the time.

But I hadn't hired in that fashion since the start of the company. At the core of our work, what we were doing at Seeker Health was so new that there really weren't experienced people to hire. And if they were, they were too expensive and risk-averse to join a fragile startup.

Instead, I looked to hire what I call "blank slates"—people who were excited, capable, and willing to learn this new trade. I looked for grit—would this person persevere in the face of obstacles? I looked for a growth mindset—can this person learn and grow? I looked for empathy—can this person relate with compassion to people with rare disease, and those trying to enroll them in clinical trials?

This interaction with Caroline was full of promise—the promise to not only continue to hire blank slates but also to use my startup, Seeker Health, to break through the traditional hiring stereotype. Also, in the realm of hiring, nothing could be more worthwhile than using my business to on-ramp a capable woman who was wishing to return to the workforce.

When I met Sharon in person, I instantly understood what Caroline had meant. First of all, Sharon had excellent work experience prior to taking her break to raise children. Also, she radiated willingness and warmth. Sharon was lit up about our mission of making clinical trials more accessible to patients and accelerating the development of critical treatments. She was willing to learn this business.

But the most important quality that I detected in Sharon was empathy. When I pictured Sharon in a customer interaction, something I've taken to doing with all of our new hires, I pictured that she would work to understand the problems and delight the customer with our solutions and with the interaction.

Furthermore, I looked to hire team members who balanced my style. Sharon had a calm and conscientious demeanor, a good offset to my fire.

I hired Sharon during the first year of Seeker Health's life and coached her to learn the job, which grew and changed over time. Since then, we have experienced a true win-win situation. Sharon has had an engaging job with a flexible schedule, and in return she has delighted customers and been instrumental in the development of our software. She is still with the company today, playing a senior role in our implementation team.

Many founders would've passed Sharon over in favor of uninterrupted work experience. Many founders would've hired three full-time employees instead of a capable part-time one. Those founders would've missed out.

THE TEACHING: GROWTH MINDSET, MISSION, AND BALANCE

The first few employees become your new family, who are enabling the growth of your startup. These first employees are critically important. In *Traversing the Traction Gap*, Bruce Cleveland agrees that your expectation might be for "... CEOs and/or founders to say that product is everything. If so, you would be wrong. The fact is, you can't win with product unless you are supported by good people, a clear customer focus, and a path to profit, revenue, and growth." It's no accident that Cleveland mentions people first.

Ultimately, employment is an exchange of value, and that value isn't always money. In lieu of traditional hiring rules such as a focus on prior experience, fancy degrees, and "can you work all day and all night long" assessment, consider focusing on building a team with the ability to learn, grow, persevere, delight customers, and balance your behaviors.

WHAT TO SEEK IN YOUR TEAM

First, look for a growth mindset. In *Mindset: The New Psychology of Success*, Carol Dweck addresses two mindsets: fixed versus growth. A "fixed mindset" assumes that we are born with our talent, skills, character, and creativity and that these traits can't be changed in any meaningful way. A "growth mindset" is the belief that all of these traits can be improved and cultivated through practice and deliberate effort.

Individuals with a growth mindset believe in their own power to change and improve, tend to be more passionate about learning, and view failures as an opportunity to improve. In contrast, those with a fixed mindset believe they can't change and typically fulfill that prophecy. They are hungry for approval, and give up when things don't work out quickly.

Here are a few attitudes a potential team member with a growth mindset will convey:

- I have the capacity to learn and grow.
- I see failures as opportunities to learn.
- I'm good at this skill because I worked hard to develop it.
- I'm willing to take action to get better.
- I welcome challenges because they help me learn.
- I appreciate feedback because it helps me become better.
- I'm a work in progress.

To some extent, it doesn't really matter what the person did before, as long as they are willing and able to learn what is in front of them now.

Second, look for a belief in your startup's mission. You want to be answering this basic question: Is this person fired up about what your company is trying to achieve? Note that this is a "yes" or "no" question. Just like in a consent conversation, a "maybe" to this question means "no."

Here are a few questions to assess a person's belief in your startup:

- Does this person appear engaged with your startup at all levels—mind, heart, body, soul?
- Does this person exhibit interest and curiosity by asking relevant questions?
- Would this person consider working at your startup a meaningful thing to do with their precious time and life?
- When a challenge arises, will this person eventually find a way to keep going because what we are working on deserves this commitment?

Third, look for balancing behaviors. Seek to balance your behavior and eventually that of the entire team, and look for an energy output that's centered, neither spilling nor withholding. Let's look at these two approaches in detail.

Balancing Behaviors with the Everything DiSC®[6]

The Everything DiSC® profile is a nonjudgmental tool used for discussion of people's behavioral differences. While we can all grow and flex, we begin with a certain behavioral style. The first step to creating a balanced team is to understand your own behavioral profile. DiSC® places people into one of four quadrants in a circle.

---

6. Everything DiSC® © 2014 by John Wiley & Sons. Everything DiSC® is a registered trademark of John Wiley & Sons. All rights reserved. Permission to reprint granted by John Wiley & Sons. For more information on Everything DiSC®, please visit www.everythingdisc.com.

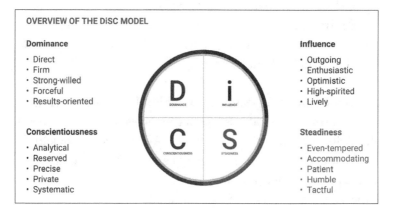

- **Top left: Dominance (D)** A person who is a D places emphasis on accomplishing results, the bottom line, and confidence.
- **Top right: Influence (i)** A person who is an i places emphasis on influencing or persuading others, openness, and relationships.
- **Bottom left: Steadiness (S)** A person who is an S places emphasis on cooperation, sincerity, and dependability.
- **Bottom right: Conscientiousness (C)** A person who is a C places emphasis on quality, accuracy, expertise, and competency.

After taking the Everything DiSC® assessment, if you discover you are an iD style that seeks to influence or persuade others and confidently drive action forward toward results, you would want to make a few hires that balance you, by having a style represented in the bottom two quadrants. Each style is fraught with a few blind spots, so hiring those with an opposite style can ensure someone will see what you are less likely to see—that somebody thinks in a way that you are less likely to think.

Guess what? Sharon's DiSC profile, which she took years after I first hired her on intuition alone, turned out to be a C, which is a perfect opposing, behavioral balance to my iD style. Proof for what I already knew.

Energy Disposition: Spilling, Withholding, or Centered
The next method to assess balance involves reading the energy disposition of the other person. Dr. Alison Ash, a sociologist who led a workshop at a SoulPlay Festival on this topic, notes that a person's energy may be in one of three states at any given time: spilling, withholding, or centered.

> **Spilling.** A person who is spilling energy is overenthusiastic. They appear a tad too hungry for this job or interaction. The recipient of this energy feels overwhelmed by the spill and generally retreats to create a more comfortable distance.

> **Withholding.** A person who is withholding energy is apathetic. They appear disengaged and distant. The recipient of this energy feels too much distance with this person, and either attempts to reengage the person or retreats completely.

> **Centered.** A person whose energy is centered is neither spilling nor withholding. They exhibit an open and welcoming demeanor. The recipient of the energy is able to stay centered, feeling neither the need to engage more nor retract.

You can use the data you collect from the interview process interactions and your intuition to make your best guess as to whether this person would balance your style and approach the role with centered energy. When I look back at some of the team members who haven't worked out for Seeker Health, they've tended to be overenthusiastic energy spillers. These folks have too much energy, it spills, becomes unfocused, and overwhelms the recipient—customers and team members. As the company grows and you begin to create larger teams, you can continue to use this tool to ensure managers are also in balance with their teams. Research shows that while diverse groups of people working on a task that can be objectively measured reported less confidence in their performance and perceived their interactions as less effective, they performed better than groups that were more homogeneous.[7] The pain of creating a diverse team and enduring the initial discomforts that may arise will be worth the gain.

Finally, keep your team small. The first question most people will ask you as your company begins to grow is how big your company is, referring to the number of employees you've hired, as if more is better.

As a startup founder, you'll feel pressure to grow your team as large and as fast as possible. Resist the pressure to overbuild your team. More is not better.

A smaller team has many benefits:

- Team members have larger and more engaging jobs, exposing them to more customers, functions, opportunities, and challenges.
- Customer interaction is more streamlined when there are only a few team members involved in that customer's work.
- Smaller teams are more open to automation because they understand that the human resource is limited.

---

7. Katherine W. Phillips, Katie A Liljenquist, and Margaret A. Neale, "Is The Pain Worth the Gain? The Advantages and Liabilities of Agreeing with Socially Distinct Newcomers," *Personality and Social Science Bulletin* 35, no. 3, (March 2009): 336–50, https://doi.org/10.1177%2F0146167208328062.

- Communication flows better.
- Payroll is smaller.
- Revenue per employee is higher.
- Profit per employee is higher.
- Runway is longer.

As in most aspects I described, you are trying to find a middle path—not too overstaffed, not too understaffed—so that your startup can have the adequate human power to thrive.

Final words: Hire to the needs of your startup—not a formula. And know that these needs will evolve as your startup grows.

GUIDED MEDITATION:
VALUE IN EACH TEAM MEMBER

Take a deep breath. Bring your energy back into your body. One more breath, and now bring your awareness to your heart. How open is it right now?

I'd like to share with you a story about my aunt, whom I called Tia Clara. One of my earliest memories is being told that Tia Clara was "not normal." Though no one could pinpoint an exact diagnosis, Tia Clara was visibly developmentally delayed. She couldn't quite retain information, or graduate from high school, and didn't have a job.

Out of necessity, my mother gave her a job. Tia Clara's job was to be there for my brothers and me after school, when my mom was at work. Tia Clara's job was to take us to the park and buy us pastries at the corner bakery, while we helped her count the change she got back. Tia Clara had a job. Her job was to love us. This has caused me to wonder the following: If my Tia Clara could maintain a job and do it so well, what does that mean for everyone else in the world?

Let's travel into your heart. I'd like to ask you this: What societal molds have been erected inside your heart? How are these molds keeping people out? How are these molds preventing you from seeing the value in each person?

Now, let's walk up to one of these molds. Maybe this is the mold that says that a person needs to work continuously, without any detours, in order to be of hiring value. Or maybe this is the mold that says that a person must have an Ivy League degree in order to work at your startup. Perhaps you are predisposed to favor people who can work all the time. Begin to investigate the types of people that you've rejected because of this mold.

Take a deep breath.

Now I'd like you to question what it would take to dismantle this mold in your heart. You decide if it stays or if it goes.

Take a deep breath into your heart, your more open heart. You decide which molds get to live in it.

And you decide whether to open your heart to see value in each person in front of you.

TL;DR

—

- As you evaluate candidates for roles at your startup, seek a willingness to grow and a passion for your mission.
- The people you hire should demonstrate the ability to grow, learn from failure, and have a tendency to value work and perseverance more than innate talent.
- Take the DiSC® assessment to understand your behavior tendencies, and use it as a guide to hire people to balance your behavior.
- Evaluate candidates' energy, looking for centered energy, neither spilling nor withholding.
- Keep your team small to maximize efficiency and sustainability.

CHAPTER 8

CLOSED DOORS SHOW YOU THE WAY

The desire for more positive experience
is itself a negative experience.
And, paradoxically, the acceptance
of one's negative experience
is itself a positive experience.
—Mark Manson, *The Subtle Art of Not Giving a F*ck*

You can't give up your passion if
things don't work right away.
You can't lose heart, or grow cynical
if there are twists and turns on your journey.
—Barack Obama

TALE FROM THE TRENCHES

Ya va a pasar. In Spanish, that means "this will soon pass," and this was my father's favorite phrase for consoling humans in any type of pain. If my brother fell down and was recoiling from pain—*ya va a pasar.* If my aunt was upset she couldn't find a job—*ya va a pasar.* If a customer of his hardware store confided in him how tough it was to make ends meet—*ya va a pasar.*

Over time, I've come to understand the phrase beyond its initial simple optimism into something more profound: all is shifting around us at all times, and while the cause of the pain may not shift, something else does that enables some relief. For the parent who loves and would do anything for their child with a rare genetic disease, the disease may never disappear, but something else may shift—a new treatment is developed, new support is found, and the obstacle is endured and, sometimes, even appreciated.

In the midst of building Seeker Health, I wished my father were alive to tell me in his own sweet voice that the frustration I often felt would also soon pass; but since he wasn't alive, I told this phrase to myself, time and time again, knowing that some of it would pass, and some of it just had to be endured.

A series of unfortunate events helped me dig deeper into the nature of difficulties. First came a complaint from a patient advocacy group regarding data collection. Bam! That's the sound of a door slamming in my face. *This will soon pass.* Next came a miscommunication with a new customer for our expansion opportunity operating under a different brand than Seeker Health. Bam! *This will soon pass.* Finally, I received a cease-and-desist letter letting me know that the name of our service was too close to the name of another service company. Bam! Bam! Bam! *This will soon pass?* I started to wonder.

Thankfully, none of these rejections were directly related to Seeker Health. These doors were slamming on a second pilot product I had decided to try out. I had thought if anyone could take some doors closed in her face for a pilot project, it would be me. But here I was, on the floor panting for air, asking myself, "Where did I go wrong, and how do I make this pain stop?"

I knew how I got here: as the clinical trials business continued to grow at a fast clip, I was growing in confidence. Finding so many untapped opportunities in the biopharmaceutical market to leverage our approach to patient finding, I identified a different need and went for it. As a pilot with inherent risk, I made the call to operate this project under a completely different brand than Seeker Health. This was possibly the only good decision I made in this short detour.

Within a month of launching this pilot, the three doors slammed in my face. I don't mind obstacles. I've dealt with many since starting Seeker Health, including late payments by customers, lengthy legal agreement turnaround times, software bugs, and quality assurance issues.

These slammed doors felt different. They felt heavy, metallic, with complicated locking mechanisms. These weren't mere obstacles that could be overcome with an apology, a new feature, or better execution. These closed doors were pointing to foundational product/market fit issues that would require a tectonic plate shift, not a new strategy. These closed doors worried me to my core that they would lead to ruined relationships and burned bridges. Like a kick in the gut and a punch in the face, these closed doors hurt. These closed doors read like neon-yellow signs, saying "Not This Way."

I'm not going to tell you that these closed doors were the best thing that ever happened to me and my startup—I can't quite get there after the pain I felt. But what I *can* say is that these closed doors were helpful, in the way a painful surgery can be, and they were instructional. These closed doors were helpful because they redirected me back to the clinical trial product that was working well, without cease-and-desist letters, disappointed customers, or bruises on my face. It wasn't time to expand, and certainly not in the direction of this pilot. Instead, it was time to stay focused and go deeper. Instead of dividing attention, Seeker Health found my single deep focus once again to continue to grow and deliver on our mission.

These closed doors were instructional in that they helped me distinguish between an obstacle and a closed door, taught me to expect both to happen throughout the process, and I learned how to resume building after encountering either one.

THE TEACHING: GOOD NEWS, BAD NEWS, WHO KNOWS?

A farmer gets a horse, which soon runs away.
A neighbor says, "That's bad news."
The farmer replies, "Good news,
bad news, who knows?"
The horse comes back and brings
another horse with him.
"Good news!" said the people.
"Good news, bad news, who knows?" replied the farmer.
The farmer gives the second horse to his son, who
rides it, then is thrown and badly breaks his leg.
"So sorry for your bad news," says
the concerned neighbor.
"Good news, bad news, who knows?" the farmer replies.
A week later, the emperor's commanders come and
take every able-bodied young man to fight in a war.
The farmer's son is spared.
—Chinese proverb

Simply, please expect perceived difficulties. Unpleasant experiences and pain are a given in startups. You'll certainly face experiences you deem as negative. Being able to differentiate the negative experiences you face will help you make the most of the opportunity.

First, you'll face obstacles. Obstacles are problems that stand in your way. These problems are solvable. Some may require more time and attention, but a solution is on the horizon. Obstacles make your startup better. Overcome them and you may find yourself gaining a new superpower that's valuable to your market.

Then, you'll face closed doors. These will resemble a brick wall, barring passage, begging you to redirect your energy. Closed doors are less simple to solve. Yes, you may eventually be able to open this closed door, but the investment of time, effort, or money is prohibitive at this time. Closed doors feel as if they weaken you and your startup. Closed doors beg you to redirect your efforts.

Determining whether a problem you face is an obstacle or a closed door is critically important to a startup. Here is a cheat sheet on how to differentiate the two.

ATTRIBUTE	OBSTACLES	CLOSED DOORS
Definition of the Problem	Something that stands in the way	A structure that bars passage
Ability to Resolve Problem	Medium to high	Low to very low
Visual Cue of the Problem	Hurdle	Brick wall
After an Attempt to Deal with the Problem	You become stronger.	You become weaker.
Message This Problem Brings to You	You can overcome obstacles. You will grow and prosper.	You can redirect your efforts. You will grow and prosper.

You don't know what today's event means in the grand scheme of things.

You don't know the final outcome, which, in essence, is ever evolving. Therefore, an event that might seem very negative can turn into a positive experience by sparing you in a way that you are unable to understand in this moment. All in all, welcome negative experiences in the form of both obstacles and closed doors. Use the obstacles to improve your startup. Use closed doors to redirect your flow.

Research supports that this ability to persevere in the face of obstacles is even more important than talent. In *Grit: The Power of Passion and Perseverance*, Angela Duckworth notes that "no matter the domain, the highly successful . . . not only had determination, they had *direction*. It was this combination of passion and perseverance that made high achievers special. In a word, they had grit." This grit is even more important than talent.

Research also supports that we learn and retain more when situations are difficult. In two separate studies, participants were divided into two groups; one group received materials in a hard-to-read font, while the other group received materials in an easy-to-read font. Two separate studies explored the extent to which this deeper processing engendered by the harder-to-read font could lead to improved memory performance. Study 1 found that information in hard-to-read fonts was better remembered than easier-to-read information in a controlled laboratory setting. Study 2 extended this finding to high school classrooms.[8] When things get harder, participants seemed to enlist more brainpower, resulting in improved memory performance.

From a mindful perspective, you can look at whatever happens during the time of your startup as grounds for growth. Events that are constructive, regardless of whether they're

8. Connor Diemand-Yauman, Daniel M. Oppenheimer, and Erikka B. Vaughan, "Fortune Favors the Bold (and the Italicized): Effects of Disfluency on Educational Outcomes," *Cognition* 118, no. 1 (January 2011): 111–115, https://doi.org/10.1016/j.cognition.2010.09.012.

under your control, are grounds for growth. Events that are destructive, regardless of whether they're under your control, are grounds for growth.

From this mindful perspective, as long as you are acting from a place of clean and clear intentions, you can't fail, you can't bomb, and you can't flop. Your clean and clear intentions for manifesting your potential are understood by the universe, and it is as if it deploys a safety net right under you. Each time you fall, as long as you learn and grow, flex and adjust, and want to carry on, you certainly will.

Allow me to clarify that you are not to test the universal safety net with trickery. Yes, if you run across the highway while all five lanes of traffic are flowing, you will be killed. There is no universal safety net that could save you from that level of stupidity. This is not how this spiritual concept works.

Your intentions must be clean and clear. You need to want to survive and grow, to serve and create. Only then has the universe an opportunity to give you another chance.

Finally, know that while facing an obstacle or a closed door, your mind will distract you with an unending supply of questions:

- Why is this happening to me?
- Should I keep going?
- Is this worth it?
- Why not quit now?
- Would it be better to consider these sunk costs?
- Could it be that my old boss wasn't that bad to work for after all?

Ignore these questions, and resolve this natural and expected resistance. You've come too far, and it's time to keep going.

GUIDED MEDITATION:
A REFLECTION ON NEGATIVE EXPERIENCES

For this meditation, you may want to have a piece of paper to journal the insights you gain.

Close your eyes. Take a deep breath. Bring back into your body all the energy that may be occupied in activities that are outside of your body. One more breath; hold it for four seconds, and as you breathe out, release any and all remaining distractions. Here you are, simply present in this moment.

In this state of inner awareness, begin to scan your life for what you may have called "negative experiences." You may have accumulated quite a few by now: disappointments, heartbreaks, and losses. Now pick one of these alleged negative experiences. Whatever it is that happened, you probably felt alone, scared, shocked, or confused in this experience.

I'd like to invite you to see this negative experience as a wave in the ocean. The wave begins to form, it grows, it peaks, then it retreats, and then it's gone. As the wave of negative feelings leaves you, what has remained of this experience? Were you strengthened by having overcome this obstacle? What did you learn? How were you redirected? You are clearly still alive and striving.

Are you able to see these negative experiences as part of the fabric of any life experience? They are normal. They are expected. And they bring gifts to harvest.

Take a deep breath and open your eyes.

TL;DR

———

- Make peace with encountering obstacles and closed doors—they are both expected along the startup way.
- An obstacle is difficult but not impossible to surmount. You can detect an obstacle because overcoming it makes you stronger or gives you a new ability.
- A closed door is so difficult to surmount that it weakens you.
- Learn to understand the difference between an obstacle and a closed door to find your focus and move forward.

CHAPTER 9

YOUR BEST EFFORT IS NEVER BURNOUT

*You have this frail vessel called the
human body that's limited on Earth.*
—Neil deGrasse Tyson

Mr. Duffy lived a short distance from his body.
—James Joyce, *Dubliners*

TALE FROM THE TRENCHES

The only reason I didn't burn out while creating Seeker Health is that I had already done so before. My prior burnout experience was so unpleasant, with so much collateral damage, that I had been forewarned.

Let's go back to 2012. I'm in Marin General Hospital in the surgery recovery room. "That sack was ready to explode. You are lucky to be alive," says the surgeon to me after removing my gallbladder and all of its stones.

Stress, pregnancies, and cleanses are among the risk factors for gallstones, and I had been a repeat customer for all three. Back then, I was working a stressful corporate job with lots of travel. Stress? Check. I had two little kids. Pregnancies? Check, check. And I was obsessed with my weight. Cleanses? Check, check, check.

I felt like a black cloud had swallowed me up whole; everything in my path—past, present, and future—looked dark. Occasionally, after a good night of sleep, I would gain an instant of awareness that I should feel grateful for having a job, and children, and such an abundant life to make me feel this tired, but that shift felt unfathomable.

The gallbladder turned out to be the symptom, not the true disease. As I began to recover from surgery, the harder work was ahead. I tried everything one who wants to get better can try: a lot of doctor's appointments, massage, acupuncture, yoga, hot yoga, Reiki, supplements, and therapy. One doctor suggested magnesium. Another, progesterone. Another, a high-protein diet. Another, a fat-free, meat-free diet. Another recommended I take "a dusting of an antidepressant to get through this rough patch," diagnosing what I had as an "adjustment disorder."

And then one day, as I was getting tired of visiting more and more people while carrying an imaginary cardboard sign saying "YOU help ME," I finally understood my disease. My disease was ME. Somehow, somewhere, I had become a workaholic and a perfectionist. Somehow, I had stopped caring for myself. Somewhere, I had lost the joy for life. Somehow, I had become maladjusted in my own life. The only one who could fix this mess was me.

To deal with this maladjustment, two logical options remained:

- Transform my life, or . . .
- Accept what was in it.

In 2014, I chose both: a lot of transformation, and a lot of acceptance. It's sometimes easier to make changes than to adjust to reality, and so I changed jobs and moved houses. Our kids moved schools; my husband and I reset our relationship, and we secured more reliable childcare. I changed the way we spent our weekends, and instead of running around all day, I made time for a nap.

I spent more time going inward, finding wounds I didn't even know were inside me. I discovered I've been feeling "not enough" ever since I'd been questioned about why I got a 98 on a test when 100 was clearly the perfect grade. I discovered resentment over my tiny ears being pierced as an infant without my express consent. I discovered old regrets over unsaid goodbyes when I left Uruguay at age sixteen, and that two decades later, I still struggled with not being given a choice about immigration, not knowing where I belong or where to call home, and not being capable of feeling abundance.

I call this totality of issues to deal with my "pain soup." My pain soup, which had been simmering for decades, with life adding ingredients here and there, was now bubbling and boiling with such force that it wasn't burning only me but others as well.

Going so deep into myself was painful. A part of me could see that this was spilled milk at this point, but someone had to mop the spill, and that someone was me. With such a backlog of issues, it was hard to pick a place to start, but I just started with whatever seemed to be triggered at any particular time. Immigration, poverty, gender discrimination, traumatic injuries—all of these ping-ponged inside me.

Albeit painful, this inner journey was also fruitful. Once I could face these painful emotions and feel them, I began to connect to me, the real me, to figure out purpose and value in my life. Finding meaning in the pain meant finding peace.

My purpose in life was to blaze trails and stitch a safety net for our family. My purpose in life was to work, to learn, and to teach. My purpose was to create a company that had an impact on real people and employed others. My purpose in life was to mother two children with unconditional love, to learn from my relationship with my husband, and to offer my life learnings to those who can use them. My purpose in life was to create from pain, create in pain—waiting for it to pass might take a lifetime.

In 2015, when the opportunity to start Seeker Health came, I took it, and I made myself a promise: I would work hard, of course, but I would not burn out ever again in my life. I had already found my human limit.

I went on to start and build. The days were busy, my brain was filling up fast, and my shoulders and jaw were beginning to lock up. It didn't take long for me to flirt with burnout: just one more client meeting, one more review of the patent filing, one more look at résumés.

Despite knowing my limits, I still flirt with burnout. Early in the year 2019 I posted this on Facebook:

> My mind has no patience for the amount of rest my body requires. And so, my mind wins the little battles of overworking when already tired, overcommitting when I'm already full, over-seeking when I've already found. But my body always, always wins the war, and I end up flat on my back until it figures out how to manufacture new energy. This poor body will one day lose this war, and that, my friends, will be forever. So, I'm going back to bed.

I continue to learn how to deal with the parts of me that want to push hard all the time. I journal, meditate, write, dance, or read inspiring material. I have loving relationships. I take time to rest and retreat.

Nowadays, I live fine without my gallbladder, a casualty of my previous stress cycle. And I also know that I'm running out of disposable body parts to sacrifice to burnout.

THE TEACHING: IMMUNIZE
YOURSELF AGAINST BURNOUT

You will have to work hard for your startup. There's no way around it. This labor is no different than laboring a new human into the world. There will be chaos. There will be pain. There will be blood. Your goal is to sustain this chaos without getting burned out.

Where's your limit? Only you know. And this is why you might need to brush up against burnout in order to avoid getting into bed with it. To sustain the frenzy of creating a new company, you will have to place value on your very human body, which requires mindful care.

Consider the obvious and the less obvious as it relates to taking care of your body.

THE OBVIOUS:

- Sleep
- Movement
- Fuel
- Hydration
- Sunlight
- Nature

Great books and resources already exist on these topics, and you'll find a few of my favorites in the section toward the back of this book titled "Resources for Continued Growth."

THE LESS OBVIOUS:

Differentiate the Stressor from Stress

In *Burnout: The Secret to Unlocking the Stress Cycle,* Emily and Amelia Nagoski help us with a key concept for protecting your vessel for creation, and that is to differentiate between the originating source of stress and the response your body will mount toward it.

- **Stressors** are what activate the stress response in your body. This may be work, a caretaking relationship, a romantic relationship, a project to start or finish, a challenging experience, your finances, and so on.
- **Stress** is the neurological and physiological shift that happens in your body and mind when you encounter a stressor.

This difference is important, because many times we manage to get rid of the stressor—the presentation ends, the contract is won, we quit the job, the semester ends, we end the relationship, the kids move out, or the paycheck comes in—but the stress response may not yet be complete, and your body and mind may still need tools to return to safety.

In startup land, the stressors remain for a long time. It takes years and decades to build a company, and thus the question becomes what to do in order to complete the stress cycle week after week, month after month, year after year. Well, read on.

Pay Attention to Your Feelings

I can tell what you are thinking: *This is a book about startups— why are we talking about feelings?!* Indeed, I'm going to spend the next few pages talking about feelings, because you are a human being, and whether you like it or not, you have feelings!

Feelings affect you, what you think you can do, and what you actually end up doing. In short, feelings affect your mindset, and therefore they require your attention.

Feelings are inevitable reactions to circumstances, with emphasis on two points: first, the inevitable nature of the reaction, and then the dependence on circumstances.[9] Both the reaction and the circumstances are impermanent. Repressing feelings or forgetting to address them isn't a clever way to protect your vessel for creation.

Instead, you want to welcome your feelings, decode the wisdom they may bring, and move on to your intention to create. Though you may feel as if only negative feelings require your attention, this isn't quite right.

In the ultracompetitive culture of startups, finding a place, person, or space to celebrate the great things that you are creating, without appearing to be a self-promoting braggart, requires a mindful approach.

So, let's start with situations in which your needs are met, and you feel relieved, joyful, grateful, maybe even delighted. These feelings last longer and penetrate your being more deeply when they are properly celebrated. Who can truly hold space for your elation? Who can help you celebrate without asking themselves why this isn't happening to them too? Where could you document these wins, in case you need to refer to them later?

What about situations in which your needs are not met, and you feel confused, embarrassed, depressed, cranky, horrified, or angry? Take a moment to mourn the situation, feel the emotion, and connect to the unmet need for you. It's absolutely allowed to feel the way you do. And emotions are, thankfully, completely temporary.

---

9. Fredric Neuman, MD, "The Purpose of Feelings," *Psychology Today* (blog), December 19, 2012, https://www.psychologytoday.com/sg/blog/fighting -fear/201212/the-purpose-feelings.

Let's do a bit of planning here. In the following table, you have an opportunity to begin to create a plan for connecting to the human beings who may be able to hold space for you to celebrate or mourn. There might be people who will prove to be exceptional at both, and others who may be better friends for mourning than for a celebration.

First, come up with a few names for each category of celebration and mourning. Then begin to investigate their availability of time and place, and finally decide if you'd like to do this on a mutual basis (you talk for fifteen minutes and the other person talks for fifteen minutes).

PLAN FOR CELEBRATION AND MOURNING

	Humans who can help me celebrate		Humans who can help me mourn	
Come up with a few names	Sue	Bob	Joel	Olivia
Best time to connect	Available mornings	Available lunch and evenings	Available evenings	Available mornings and lunch
Best place to connect	Phone	Walk, coffee, phone	Phone	Walk, coffee
Establish mutuality	Interested	Interested	Not interested	Interested

If you are tentative on this, then listen to the research on oxytocin—this is the neurotransmitter that's released during sex, childbirth, and lactation, sometimes nicknamed the "bonding hormone." When released, oxytocin produces feelings of well-being, relaxation, trust, and psychological stability.[10] Now get this: when we share our feelings with a friend, fully clothed, in a completely nonsexual, nonromantic situation, oxytocin is also released![11]

Let's go deeper still to the bottom of your pain soup.
If you feel like I felt in 2012, and your pain soup of past losses, resentments, and disappointments has been simmering on the stove for years and it's beginning to boil over, you might be best served by a deliberate mindful attempt to address your pain soup.

Your pain soup may have begun simmering in childhood. This is one of the reasons why "tell me about your mother or father" (say it in a Freudian accent) is a good place to start for therapists. The unfortunate reality is that the vast majority of us do not cross into adulthood with an empty pain cauldron. According to author Sara Wiseman, trauma from family of origin comes in seven types:[12]

1. Abuse
2. Addiction
3. Violence
4. Poverty
5. Illness

10. Markus MacGill, "What Is the Link between Love and Oxytocin?" *Medical News Today*, September 4, 2017, https://www.medicalnewstoday.com/articles /275795.php.

11. Judith E. Glaser, "Psychology of Deep Connection," *Psychology Today* (blog), September 29, 2015, https://www.psychologytoday.com/us/blog/conversational -intelligence/201509/psychology-deep-connection.

12. Sara Wiseman, "Release Yourself from Family Karma," *DailyOM*, (2020): https://www.dailyom.com/cgi-bin/courses/courseoverview.cgi?cid=490.

6. Abandonment
7. Betrayal

Childhood is a time when we are entitled to protection and nurturing. When, instead of receiving this safety and nourishment, one or more of the shadows above are present, they affect us in a profound way and for the rest of our lives. In adulthood, we may repeat what we saw in childhood, or we swing to the other extreme of the pendulum, or we attempt to actually heal. Some of the trauma you may be able to address on your own, and some may require the help of a therapist or professional to feel and overcome these powerful emotions in a safe way.

There are several hopeful aspects to these shadows: First, once you decide to feel your pain—to face it, to examine it—it begins to pass. Next, you aren't alone; by the time we cross into adulthood, all of us have been exposed to some pain. Pain is the magma of the human experience.

SO, WHAT DO YOU DO WITH ALL THIS PAIN?
Here's your checklist. Your job is:

- To become aware of your pain
- To identify the coping mechanisms you enacted to deal with your pain
- To accept that you can create, from pain, while still in pain

Let's work with these one at a time.

Your first job is to become aware of your pain. I deliberately listed the seven shadows above as a starting inventory for your internal experience. For example, if I were to identify my trauma around immigration, I would say that during this time I experienced the abrupt loss of "home" and important

relationships, immediate poverty, and stood witness to a tad
too much physical violence toward my own family members
(circa 1992–93, Brooklyn, New York).

QUESTIONS FOR YOU:
What or who has caused you pain? What type of pain?

Your second job is to identify the coping mechanisms you
enacted to deal with this pain. A coping mechanism is an
adaptation to stress, which you create to enhance your control over the situation. Because a coping mechanism can often
be subconscious, many of us struggle to become aware of our
own adaptations. For example, only after years of introspec-
tion did I figure out that my coping mechanism to deal with
the pain of immigration has been outward accomplishment.
This coping mechanism helped me gain control over poverty,
enter environments where physical safety was more assured
(universities, corporations), and forget about my pain of feeling
"homeless" inside. Once I can see my coping mechanism, I can
realize that which was once adaptive is now getting in my way,
and in this recognition I can begin to heal.

QUESTIONS FOR YOU:
What adaptations have you made in your life to control the
result of your pain? How are these coping mechanisms working
out for you?

Your third and most important job is to accept that you can
create in pain. You need not wait until some unknown time in
the future when you are "unbroken" or "healed," as that level
of perfection may never manifest. Instead, you create now, a
little broken, still quite unhealed, and aware of your pain. For
example, I turned my immigration odyssey into a memoir (not
yet published). And furthermore, during the creation of Seeker

Health, I felt powered by the pain over the loss of my father just a few months before I started the company—his body hadn't allowed him to become an entrepreneur in the United States, but mine would.

QUESTIONS FOR YOU:
Is pain stopping you from creating? Have you created in pain before? What creation may emerge from the pain you feel now?

Now that you have felt your feelings, do not let them overtake you. Feelings are just that: feelings. They come, they bring messages, they go, they come again.

Set clear intentions for what you seek to accomplish in the world *despite* your feelings. Let's say your intention is to build your startup and acquire fifty more customers, but right now you are feeling frustrated about an interaction you had with customer number ten. Feel the frustration, and determine whether there's anything that can be solved or learned. Then return to your intention. Remember, you wanted to acquire fifty customers. Keep going.

Surround Yourself with Close Others Who Believe in You
The founder's role is a lonely job. While you may be happy being alone a lot of the time, you are a social animal of the human kind. That means that you have at least a few of these needs:

- Companionship
- Partnership
- Friendship
- Reassurance
- Closeness
- Intimacy
- To be seen

- To be heard
- To be known
- Stimulation
- Touch
- Sex
- Love

Having some or all of these needs doesn't render you needy. It makes you just like everyone else. These needs are generally met through other people. Since you are already in a demanding relationship with your startup, there will be little room for relationships that are not a net positive for you. So, choosing the "close others" requires mindfulness.

Research corroborates that close others who believe in you and your achievement of your goal can increase your motivation and actual performance toward that goal. At the University of Wisconsin–Madison,[13] researchers led by James Shah designed five separate studies to evaluate the impact of close others on task performance. Their consistent results showed that those who felt close to a significant other (mother, father, sibling, partner, etc.) who was supportive of the task (getting a good test score) performed better on the task when primed with the role of this close other. If primed with an image of a person who wasn't "close" or didn't support the task, performance didn't improve. In simpler terms, let's assume that you are sitting to take the GMAT, you are close to your mother, and your mother believes you should pursue your MBA; then this research would say that priming yourself with an image of your mother would increase your test performance in a measurable and significant way.

---

13. E. Benson, "People More Likely to Pursue Goals After Unconscious Reminders of Friends, Relatives," *Journal of Personality and Social Psychology*, Vol. 84, No. 4, (April 2003): 661–681.

Only after reading this research (a couple of times) did I begin to understand I had been priming myself for performance throughout the creation of Seeker Health. First, I primed myself with the memory of my dead father. *Is it possible that when it comes to internal motivation, your influential close other may not even need to be alive?* Then I primed myself in the presence of close others (Phil, my mom, my brothers, my kids) with whom I live and interact and who were supportive of my entrepreneurial pursuit.

Whom you surround yourself with during this period of creation matters. Here are a few prompts to evaluate your close others.

- Do they believe in you?
- Do they want what's best for you?
- Are they supportive of your specific goal?
- Do they encourage you to keep going?
- Is there a feeling of reciprocity in the relationship?

It is time to look around to determine who stays, who goes, and who needs clearer boundaries.

Practice Retreating
Whenever you feel the urge to quit, retreat instead. Consider a retreat in a place that will support your need for rest and regeneration. A retreat is different than a traditional vacation in that the purpose isn't just a change of setting or an escape from routine. Instead, a retreat is about going to meet yourself, exactly as you are now.

Retreats offer a few important things when it comes to completing the stress response because they can offer the mental, physical, and heart space to:

- Sleep more
- Reflect on yourself
- Connect to others on a similar journey
- Make new friends
- Feel something
- Cry and mourn
- Celebrate and feel joy
- Journal
- Work on a creative project
- Be in nature
- Have someone cook meals for you
- Reset intentions
- Learn you want to keep going

See "Resources for Continued Growth" in the back of the book for my highly recommended retreat ideas.

In summary, you have only one body from which to create your startup. Treat it as the sophisticated organism that it is: observe your feelings, surround yourself with close others, and retreat when needed, and you will stand strong and productive as you create.

GUIDED MEDITATION:
EMBODIED RELAXATION

In this meditation, I will guide you to achieve a deep sense of physical, mental, and emotional relaxation. Please begin by finding a quiet place to sit or lie down. Close your eyes. Take a deep breath, and begin to imagine a warm light above the crown of your head. This is the light of deep relaxation. As it touches the crown of your head, you feel that area begin to relax. All tension in that area has been melted by this warm light of relaxation.

Now the light moves to your forehead and your eyes. They feel heavy and completely relaxed.

The light travels to your nose, cheeks, and mouth. Your jaw loosens, and your entire face feels very, very relaxed.

Please take another deep breath and invite this light to travel down your neck to your shoulders, upper back, and arms. These areas now feel completely relaxed.

The light travels down your chest, to your internal organs, lower back, and pelvis. Your entire torso is free of stress now and completely relaxed.

Now the light travels down your legs and feet. Any remaining stress leaves your body, out from your feet.

In this deep state of complete relaxation, you take a moment to honor this sacred vessel that holds your brain and your heart. Express your gratitude for your body carrying you to this present moment when you are creating such important things for the world.

Open your eyes. Wiggle your fingers and toes. And commit to your body, once more: to care for your body, to protect your body, and to honor your body.

TL;DR

- Mess with your body and your body will mess with you.
- Honor your basic needs, including sun, nourishment, sleep, and hydration, and respect the natural cycles and rhythms your body operates on.
- Find people who provide a space of unconditional acceptance for you to celebrate or despair, whether a best friend, spouse, or therapist.
- Listen to your emotions, and become aware of your pain. Accept that you are not alone in your pain, and that it is OK to create in pain.
- Human connection immunizes you against burnout. Make sure to nurture positive relationships with close others who believe in you.
- When you feel the urge to quit, retreat instead, and allow the mental, physical, and heart space to work wonders on you and propel you to the next step.

PART 3

EXIT

CHAPTER 10

ASK FOR THE REALLY GOOD STUFF (AND YOU DESERVE IT)

Like a sandcastle,
all is temporary. Build it, tend it, enjoy it.
And when the time comes, let it go.
—Jack Kornfield

If you are not enough before the gold medal,
you won't be enough with it.
—Coach Irv in the movie *Cool Runnings*

TALE FROM THE TRENCHES

I never set out on a process to deliberately exit Seeker Health. The opportunities presented themselves with such variety and force that I had no choice but to look up from building the business, and pay attention.

First, I received an email from the president of a healthcare communications firm, which I'll refer to as Company 1. The president had been a colleague of mine a decade ago. He had been tracking Seeker Health's progress in clinical trial enrollment since the start, and he expressed an interest in building his own firm in this direction.

> From: President, Company 1
> To: Sandra Shpilberg
> Can we get time for you to present your story to my private equity partners? In our offices mid-November for 90 minutes?

I replied yes, and we arranged a meeting under confidentiality. This might have been a tricky meeting. While I was concerned the company might use this meeting to learn what we were doing, copy it, and put us out of business, I trusted my former colleague was more decent than that and was actually serious about pursuing an acquisition of Seeker Health. At the meeting, I presented the Seeker Health patient-finding methods and our financial statement summary to the group he had assembled.

A few days later, the private equity partner for Company 1 sent a list of preliminary information they would like to review in order to further evaluate the opportunity to buy Seeker Health. The list was digging deeper into who our customers were, and the financial profiles of each of our contracts. Despite having more than a full-time job running the business, I responded as soon as I could with the information requested.

In November and December, Company 1 arranged for a number of meetings for me to meet their business leaders, plan joint customer pitches as a trial run, and discuss our technology stack with their CTO. These meetings took quite a bit of time away from running the business. I hired a new person to run sales, and was relying more and more on the team I had assembled to run with customer work.

Because Company 1 was partially owned by a private equity firm, the financial performance of Seeker Health really mattered. As soon as the year closed out, I sent the following email:

> From: Sandra Shpilberg
> To: Company 1 & PE Firm
> Happy new year! For your review, please find attached the following documents, updated today:
> - Income Statement
> - Final Billings by Customer
> - Forecast Income Statement and Revenue by Customer for next year (Contracted & Go-Get)

I flew east to jointly present to a potential customer. Though I didn't expect much from this early pitch, some concerns began to pop up for me. The pitch had seemed like we threw spaghetti at the wall—the meeting seemed to lack focus—but I wrote it off as a symptom of our first time presenting together.

Wanting to learn more about the mergers and acquisitions (M&A) process, I reached out to Rachel, a friend of my brother's who had recently sold a technology company, and I learned this:

- First, the buyer would produce a letter of intent (LOI), a nonbinding document that would outline the general terms of the deal.
- Then, I would assemble a team to include at least a lawyer and an accountant to review the letter and its implications.
- Once a final LOI was signed, due diligence would begin. While this may vary, at a minimum I should

expect the buyer to begin workstreams in each of the following areas:

- Financial statements
- Technology
- Customer contracts
- Human resources practices
- Vendor contracts
- Legal matters

- Somewhere toward the end of the due diligence, the buyer's legal team would draft a purchase agreement and any other agreements (such as a founder employment agreement) that may be necessary to provide to my legal team for review and negotiation.
- Once the legal agreements are mutually agreed upon, the funds would be wired on the closing date.

Rachel concluded with "Remember, the deal's not done until it is done. At any given time the buyer can pull out. Once you see all the papers signed and the wire in your account, then you know you are done." Rachel offered the clarity I needed to keep going. Next stop: LOI.

Company 1 then requested a meeting at Seeker Health's office, to meet some of our key team members and do a deep dive on our business.

This presented two great challenges for me:

First, should I tell the employees participating in this meeting about Company 1's potential and confidential interest in acquiring Seeker Health, though I didn't even have an LOI?

Second, I felt embarrassed about the small dimensions of our office at the coworking space. We had access to a shared conference room with orange chairs, which screamed "optimistic startup" loud and clear, but eventually, they would see the closet from which I was operating a multimillion-dollar company.

On the first issue, I decided to be honest with relevant employees and ask for complete confidentiality on the matter. On the second issue, I decided our current housing was a sign of our lean, efficient machine—more a point of pride than embarrassment.

A few days later, a group of about ten people from Company 1 descended upon our coworking space to learn more about Seeker Health.

At a high level, certain employees and I covered the problem we were solving, how we were solving it, who our top customers were, how we charged for our work, our technology stack, our financial performance, and plans for growth. We concluded the meeting with dinner and drinks at Joya in Palo Alto.

I returned home to all the work from the day waiting to get done, and my family, excitedly waiting for an update.

"It went well," I said. "Next stop: LOI."

The next day, one of the participants in the meeting sent me this email:

> From: Company 1 Division Leader
> To: Sandra Shpilberg
> Sandra—congratulations again on the
> last two years. So exciting to see another
> talented woman building a great business,
> and a committed mom, too! Really enjoyed
> our time together yesterday. Look forward
> to more collaboration and partnership in
> the months ahead. Please let me know
> if you want to connect at all along the
> way. You were fantastic with the PE guys
> yesterday!

This email was a great gift. "Building a great business" stood out. I was running forward all the time, and so it was a gift to have an opportunity to pause and appreciate.

With this appreciation, a question emerged for me. Yes, "next stop: LOI," but what was Seeker Health worth? When tech companies pursue funding, valuations are usually invented. In the case of Seeker Health, the business had revenue, cash flow, and profit. These were the ingredients for calculating a more precise valuation.

I retained a valuation accountant to produce an accurate calculation of Seeker Health's worth. I shared all financial information and forecasts, and set him free to crunch the numbers.

Next came this email:

> From: Company 1's PE Firm
> To: Sandra Shpilberg
> Thanks for a great meeting, Sandra. We are very excited about your business and what we might be able to accomplish together.
>
> We'll be in touch to move toward executing an LOI and also to provide a rough calendar of milestones to check off toward completing a deal in the next couple months—assuming all checks out in deeper diligence. Thanks for considering us as a partner to drive the future growth of Seeker Health.

Just like the long-faced characters in Dr. Seuss's book *Oh, the Places You'll Go!*, I was now majoring in waiting. I "headed, I fear, toward a most useless place. The Waiting Place . . ."

Waiting for a train to go
or a bus to come, or a plane to go
or the mail to come, or the rain to go
or the phone to ring, or the snow to snow
or waiting around for a Yes or No
or waiting for their hair to grow.

All is impermanent, including the time in the Waiting Place, and on a Sunday evening I received the long-awaited message from Company 1.

> From: Company 1's PE Firm
> To: Sandra Shpilberg
> Apologies for the slight delay in getting this across to you. We are pleased to present to you a draft of the LOI. The one change that I'd like to highlight is that we plan to close the transaction on April 30th to make sure we have enough time to get through all of the diligence workstreams outlined in our LOI. We are extremely excited about our combination and will plan to partner prior to close to drive new business ensuring a successful outcome for all.

I took a quick look at the LOI, smiled, told my husband, sent a quick email to the accountant requesting our valuation, and responded to Company 1 as follows:

> From: Sandra Shpilberg
> To: Company 1's PE Firm
> Great. Thank you for sending the LOI, and I'm most excited about the combination of Company 1 and Seeker Health as well.

> I will review the letter along with our
> attorney and will get back to you as soon
> as possible.

Not a minute too soon, the valuation accountant provided his recommendation. The valuation of Seeker Health on Company 1's LOI was certainly inside the range, but definitely on the lower side.

The LOI called for the expected confirmatory due diligence in the following areas: business operations, accounting, legal, clients, information systems, insurance and benefits, and management background checks.

Finally, if I signed the LOI, as was expected, I would enter an exclusivity period, whereby I could not solicit, encourage, accept, or consummate a deal to sell Seeker Health to another party.

I began to negotiate with Company 1's president to move favorably in my direction. Yet, a part of me couldn't help but think there was a much better deal out there. Because Company 1 seemed willing to negotiate in my direction, I began to assemble my deal team. Based upon a friend's recommendation, I hired a lawyer experienced in M&A deals of this size. After this lawyer's explanation of the impact of the indemnity clauses, which are meant to protect the buyer from anything that could go wrong with this purchase, and all the ways in which the buyer could try to get their money back from me, I was petrified.

I pushed through the fear. I had no time to find a new lawyer who would be more sensitive to my inherited anxiety profile. The lawyer reviewed the LOI. We went back and forth a few times with suggested changes for Company 1, and soon we had a signed LOI.

Around this time, my brother Javier reached out to find out if I wanted an introduction to an incubator to which he was connected. Just for fun, I reviewed the incubator's requirements—wanting their startups not too cold, not too hot. Seeker Health had already blown past the top of their range for revenue and profit. This startup toddler was already walking around on two solid, chunky feet—and Company 1 wanted to buy it.

As due diligence began, my workload grew exponentially. In addition to running the business, getting new clients, and onboarding new employees, I had a few part-time jobs: populating the diligence data room and having calls with accountants, lawyers, and others explaining the inner workings of Seeker Health.

During this time, *Medical Marketing & Media*, an industry publication, named me a Top 40 Healthcare Transformer. I flew to New York to collect my award and stayed at my mom's apartment. Looking through her old photo albums of our family when we were kids reminded me that there was still life outside the world of M&A into which I had now been sucked whole.

Phil was working overtime to keep me half-sane. I was sleeping no more than a few hours a night, waking up at four a.m., and shuffling to the dining room to see what emails had been sent while I was sleeping.

On one of these nights, Phil approached, holding small white bottles on each hand.

"Melatonin or Tylenol PM?" he said.

I winced, thinking there was no way I was going to turn myself off during this time.

"I know you," Phil continued. "You'll start losing your mind if you don't sleep."

With the reluctance of a child being forced to eat broccoli, I swallowed the melatonin tablet and shuffled back to bed.

The next morning, there was a predictable deluge of emails waiting for me, primarily to schedule the accountants to come on-site. In preparation, they had a list of additional items they needed me to add to the data room.

I was beginning to worry I wasn't spending enough time on new business and that our client deal flow was beginning to show the slightest note of a slowdown. *Let's get through the accounting,* I told myself. *Right after that, I'll get back on business development.*

The next week, the two accountants traveled to Seeker Health, and we bunkered down in the conference room with the orange chairs for a very long day of debits and credits. Perhaps it was because I had studied accounting for my bachelor's degree, or because I had also taken the CPA exam, or most likely because I loved the tools that accounting provided to measure a business, but we immediately established a rapport.

The two accountants took turns politely issuing requests. "We seem to be missing the contract with Client S. Do you have it?" and then "Could we have a copy of your contract with the software developer?" followed by "And how about the bill for the clinical trials conference in February?"

I was surprised when, upon being unable to produce a receipt for a $4.95 charge at the airport or recall what it was for, they both said, "We can let that one go." Anything above that amount was reviewed and reconciled, debits probed, and credits dissected. At the end of the day, they left satisfied, but not offering the closure I needed for some relief. They left it at "We'll reach out if we need anything else."

I immediately turned back to business development. Despite hiring a person to lead this function, it still very much leaned on me. We could not fall behind.

Next, something unexpected happened.

From: Representative of Company 2
To: Sandra Shpilberg
Hi, Sandra,

We represent one of the largest
privately held diversified healthcare
communications businesses in the US.
They have asked us to reach out to you
to determine if you would discuss an
acquisition by our client of your business.

A few key points about our client:

- They are mission driven and have
  revenues in excess of $100M, with high
  margins.
- One of their prime specialties is
  oncology.
- They have both media and marketing
  divisions.
- The CEO is the majority owner and
  M&A decision-maker of the business;
  senior management personally
  identified your company.

Could you let me know if you would be
willing to speak with me by phone so that I
could identify our client and tell you more
about this opportunity?

A second company was interested in acquiring Seeker
Health?! Great news, but I had signed an exclusivity agreement
with Company 1.

From: Sandra Shpilberg
To: Representative of Company 2
Thank you for your interest in Seeker
Health. At this time, I'm unable to engage

in this type of conversation. I'll reach out
should circumstances change.

The following week, Company 1 and I went on to another
joint pitch to a potential customer. Just like the first time, I
walked out thinking that the overall pitch was still unfocused
and unsuccessful. We weren't getting any better at pitching
new customers together. Even the preparation process was
chaotic. A part of me felt I shouldn't be looking for defects.
Company 1 was going to pay me for Seeker Health, and all I
had to do was survive a few years together. Another part of me
was screaming that this was not going to be tolerable.

A few days later, something even more astonishing happened. I received an unsolicited call from a person familiar
with Company 1 and Seeker Health. The person called me specifically to say that Company 1 "is a mess." I had known this
person for a long time as authentic and trustworthy. His opin-
ion mattered to me, and there was no way I could completely
dismiss his comments.

At around this time, I began the reverse due diligence. I
requested Company 1 provide their audited financial statement, revenue by client, organizational chart, and the next
year's forecast.

Despite the work intensity, I decided to spend the day
attending the Digital Health CEO Summit in San Francisco.
I'd found this conference valuable the previous year. This time,
I sat on a panel focused on burnout. The various members dis-
cussed strategies for avoiding it, such as digital-free Saturdays
and virtual assistants, and how to fit in exercise.

The topic that raised the most interest in me was the use
of an executive coach as half propeller of progress, half business therapist. A small minority of founders used an executive
coach, but those who used one appreciated their value. The
crux of the value seemed to be in having a smart, experienced

person who had been there and done that, and could help a founder sort out thoughts and achieve clarity.

This moment seemed like a great time to strive for clarity for Seeker Health. I left the summit with two coach recommendations from other founders in the room. As a grand sign from the universe, another coach, Charles Rose, reached out to me on LinkedIn. Charles had sold a software business of a similar size a few years back. I hired Charles and we got to work.

Our first main task was to clarify the following questions:

- Did I want to sell Seeker Health now?
- If the answer was yes, what were my preferred deal terms?

The next week, there was total silence from Company 1. No emails. No phone calls. No texts. No nothing. This was the first telltale sign that something was going awry. But I had a business to keep building, so I put my single deep focus into that.

A week later the silence was finally broken by Company 1, requesting a call as soon as possible. *Sure—I'll drop everything right now, so I can hear in words what my intuition already felt in gut whisperings.*

During the call, Company 1 announced their concern about Seeker Health's sales slowing and a lack of effectiveness of our joint pitches. They were suggesting that we put the deal on hold.

In response to their concerns, I noted that the deal pipeline for Seeker Health still looked robust, and I agreed that our joint pitches had been lackluster. I shared that I had received additional inbound interest on acquiring Seeker Health, which I hadn't been able to explore due to the existing exclusivity agreement. Instead of a hold on the deal, I was looking for an end to the exclusivity agreement so that I could approach Company 2.

They seemed surprised that another company was interested, but the next day, I received a letter ending the exclusivity agreement. I was now free to pursue Company 2. The same day, I typed this email:

> From: Sandra Shpilberg
> To: Representative of Company 2
> I hope this finds you well, and I'm very appreciative of your interest in Seeker Health. The time is right on my side now to further explore this opportunity. If you'd like to schedule a call, my availability is as follows.

When I paused to breathe, I was grateful for the experience with Company 1. Having never done an M&A deal before, I realized that the interactions with Company 1 now felt like an incredibly valuable dress rehearsal.

During this time, Charles and I began our work in earnest to clarify whether or not the time was right to sell Seeker Health. As part of the clarity process, Charles provided me with two tables to complete on different days.

The first table asked me to sort through the cost and payoff of selling Seeker Health that year, from an emotional, spiritual, physical, and financial perspective. The second table presented a cost-and-payoff scenario in which I continued the year building Seeker Health instead.

IF I SELL SEEKER HEALTH THIS YEAR . . .

AREA	COST	PAYOFF/ BENEFITS
Emotional	This is costing me some freedom. This is costing me some autonomy.	This provides me satisfaction that I built something valuable. This provides me internal validation. This provides me external validation. This provides me confidence.
Spiritual	This is costing me some possible regret that I sold too early.	This is a "good" end, and everything ends.
Physical	This is probably going to cost me even more time on the road, traveling as an employee during the integration period.	This provides me less stress over back-office functions to focus more on front-office (products/customers).
Financial	This is costing me any future financial growth.	This provides me financial liquidity on value built so far. This allows me to achieve the financial security goals I've set for my family.

IF I DON'T SELL SEEKER HEALTH THIS YEAR . . .

AREA	COST	PAYOFF/ BENEFITS
Emotional	This is costing me a missed opportunity to lock down some value built.	I guess I'm still working on raising this baby?
Spiritual	I continue working patiently to make something bigger. Patience is one of my spiritual growth areas.	This provides me continued autonomy.
Physical	This is costing me continued stress from being a single owner.	This provides me continued independence.
Financial	This is costing me immediate financial security.	The final financial payoff could be larger (or smaller, or none, uncertain!).

Next, we worked on the "costs" of selling Seeker Health this year to discover a way to reduce or eliminate them. For example, the cost to my freedom and autonomy might be abated by making the integration period short.

I visited Company 2 in person. This was not my first rodeo, and it seemed infinitely easier. At the meeting, Company 2 brought its owner, general manager, and investment banker. The meeting was cordial, but I wasn't sure the fit was optimal. Company 2 specialized in healthcare communication to doctors instead of patients. The acquisition of Seeker Health would be its first foray into this highly regulated area. I was beginning to see that none of these deals were going to be a perfect fit, and that I should once again strive for obtaining an LOI with concrete deal terms.

About a month later, Company 2 provided an LOI. The good news was that the valuation was higher than Company 1's. The bad news? The rest of the terms were not attractive, and I'm being vague on purpose. When I met with Charles for our biweekly call, I reviewed the situation. We celebrated the fact that in just a few months, two companies had made offers to acquire Seeker Health, and that the valuation was higher for the second. Then I mourned how untakeable Company 2's proposition was.

In our shared Google Doc, I wrote:

"I WANT THE REALLY GOOD STUFF."

And Charles made me add, "AND I DESERVE IT."

I thanked Company 2 for their offer and told them I would need a few weeks to respond. At this junction, I was trying to buy myself time. I wasn't sure exactly what would happen next, but time was a good first ingredient.

I called my brother Joel to share my disappointment. "If there were two companies interested in acquiring Seeker Health, there must be another one . . . or two or ten," he said. Then, channeling my dad, he said: "You built a jewel here," and that made me cry.

In the meantime, I continued working with Charles to identify areas to build Seeker Health. Business development needed constant attention. To free up more time for sales, I outsourced invoicing, collections, and transaction reconciliation, which were on my overflowing plate.

We spent the next week clarifying what a good deal would look like. Charles asked me: "What is the really good stuff?" to help me get clear on deals that would be ideal.

I created a list of "really good stuff" that an offer to acquire Seeker Health would have to include:

- Valuation of X or greater
- 100 percent sale of the company
- >Y percent payment at closing in cash if dealing with a private company
- <Z percent future payment, and contingent on something I could somewhat control, such as revenue
- Up to two-year employment agreement for integration
- Seeker Health stays within ten miles of current location
- All current employees continue as employees of the new entity
- Acquirer appreciates our technology and its scalability
- Acquirer relieves Seeker Health of shared functions (HR, accounting, IT services, legal, compliance, insurance)

Joel was right. A representative of Company 3 contacted me via LinkedIn to inquire about acquiring Seeker Health. Once again, he had learned about the company via his management.

We scheduled a call for an overview of Seeker Health. At the end of the call, Company 3 asked what I was looking for in an offer. Having had just sorted that out with Charles, I paraphrased the top five bullets in the "really good stuff" list.

There were no odd sounds of shock or bewilderment on the other side of the line, which served as great reinforcement to always ask for what I want. We went on to close the call with preparations for in-person meetings, one at each company's respective office.

These in-person meetings had a different feel. Company 3 seemed to understand Seeker Health from the start. This wasn't surprising: Company 3 had worked in patient communication for a long time, understood the demand for our product, and valued the scalability our software enabled.

These meetings felt right, and within a few days, Company 3 presented an LOI that overlapped with many of my requirements on the list of "really good stuff."

The next week, as I was still going about the normal activities for business building, I presented at an industry conference in Philadelphia to generate customer interest and leads. After my presentation, I was approached by a representative of Company 4. We sat at a table in the networking room, and I answered a few of his questions and asked some of my own. Then I stated: "I have an LOI in hand already, so if your company is interested, how fast can you act?" He promised to connect me to the CEO of Company 4. He did so over email a few days later, but when I replied to find time to discuss, there was no response.

I'll take a mindful pause here:

What (the heck) were these three to four companies interested in buying?

Along the way, they shared their criteria, which included:

- A business with proven traction
- A large number of customers, without significant concentration on any single one
- Monthly recurring revenue that doubles, triples, or more, year on year
- Annual profit that doubles, triples, or more, year on year
- Technology that scales

- Leadership and a team who could deliver the next level of scale
- A good product/service fit for cross-selling their current offerings

Ok, back to LOI land. The legal redlines on the LOI with Company 3 were finished, and there was no sign of Company 4. It was time to sign or stall.

I checked in with myself: Could I recognize *enough* when it was right in front of me? I knew this offer was enough, because I had made a list of what a really good offer looked like with Charles, and the offer from Company 3 cleared all parameters. I could also wait to see what Company 4 might bring, but they weren't moving very fast.

I made my decision and signed Company 3's LOI. Their offer was enough, and perhaps so was I, with or without the expected transaction and payouts.

Due diligence began, but this time around, it felt a lot easier, since Company 3 was looking for largely the same information Company 1 had requested.

All throughout due diligence, I was keeping the business development pipeline of new customer deals hot. Company 1 was wrong about a sales slowdown: between May and August, Seeker Health signed contracts with eight new customers.

A few weeks later, an assistant for the CEO of Company 4 emailed me to schedule a meeting. I responded that I was unable to meet at this time due to being under an exclusivity agreement. A few minutes after hitting Send, I received a call from the Company 4 representative who had approached me at the conference.

"Do you think our CEO has nothing to do all day but reach out to a tiny startup in Palo Alto no one has ever heard of?" he asked, irked and angry that I hadn't waited for them.

"I had an LOI in hand, as I explained when we first met, and decided to go with that," I responded, and maneuvered myself out of the call with as much grace as I could muster under the circumstances. If anything, this call reassured me that I had taken the right step not waiting for their offer.

A few weeks later, Company 3 and Seeker Health cleared through the due diligence and reverse due diligence lists, and the date of closing was now fast approaching. Purchase and employment agreements were drawn up by Company 3's legal team and sent to my lawyer, who turned out to have a long-planned vacation to Hawaii.

"George, I'm all for vacation, and I hope you have a great time, but I'll need the redlines while you're in Hawaii," I said.

"Yes, ma'am," he replied.

It was all still feeling surreal to me. The coaching time with Charles focused on keeping me centered and sane. I asked for the good stuff, I received it, and now it was time to take the deal through to the finish line, all while keeping customers delighted, acquiring new ones, planning product updates, and managing the team.

Phil was excited too now. Neither of us slept at regular intervals anymore. On those sleepless nights, Rachel's words reverberated in the back of my mind: "It's not over until the papers are signed and the wire is confirmed."

All of this work could still result in nothing.

Or it could result in more than enough.

The week after Labor Day, we were still going back and forth on pesky contract terms like net working capital, which refers to the amount of cash the buyer expects will be left in the business to continue to operate without additional infusions.

At last, all redlines were agreed upon, and we had contracts ready for execution. I drove to the office, just like any old day, except that Phil sat at the desk next to me, to watch the show.

I printed and signed in blue ink the dozen signature pages, scanned them, and sent them back. The paper part was over.

A person from Company 3's team called to verify wiring instructions one last time. I was now giddy enough to confuse an 8 with a 0, but somehow managed to read all numbers accurately.

"OK," the finance person said on the phone, "I'm about to push the wire. Please call me back when you see it on your side."

Refresh, refresh, refresh.

A dozen more times.

A call to my financial advisor.

Refresh again.

Phil calls financial advisor.

Refresh again.

There it was. The finish line to this pursuit, written in numbers.

Being enough, having enough, doing enough have been themes of struggle for me in my life. Finally, here was more than enough, not only for me but for my family, the employees of Seeker Health, our customers, and the patients we work to serve. I would stand to ensure that this feeling of abundance would ripple to all who touched and were touched by Seeker Health, as I learned to see enough when it was right in front of me. Could it be possible that I had been enough all along and just failed to see?

And, just like a beginner, I didn't know then what the integration period with Company 3 would hold. But what I knew was that I could trust my mindset to get me from this exciting end to a brand-new beginning.

THE TEACHING: ASK FOR WHAT YOU WANT

You may not know whether an entity will come tomorrow to acquire your startup, so all you can do is be prepared, just in case. A few pieces of advice:

- **Allow yourself to be found.** Targeted visibility of your startup is important. Let's focus on the word "targeted." This is the opposite of mass media. Focus on industry publications and conferences where you will find customers, suppliers, competitors, and adjacent companies. If you are striving for an acquisition, your acquirer may be venturing here too. For example, if you start a company that provides technology for digital fitting rooms, you are more likely to find your acquirer and customers at a fashion/retail industry conference, where Macy's, Nordstrom, and Bloomingdale's may be attending, than at TechCrunch Disrupt.

- **Maintain squeaky-clean records.** By the time a company comes to buy you, it's too late to clean up five years of sloppy financial records and organize all of the information requested. Hire a professional accounting firm to ensure your startup, no matter how small, engages in a monthly closing process that issues accurate financial statements. All along, maintain organized records of your formation and equity documentation. Maintain a copy of any and all contracts to which your company is a party.

- **Strive for profitability.** It is important for you to remember that outside of the alternate reality of venture capitalist funding, companies engaged in business are meant to make a profit. An acquirer is more likely to buy a business that is accretive, meaning that the income of the startup increases the income of the acquirer. Companies, of course, may also purchase startups purely for their technology, employees, users, or revenue (despite losses), but being able to turn a profit year on year reduces the risk of the acquisition for the acquirer.

Finally, a gift: a sample due diligence list, to prepare you for this stage.[14]

- Financials

    - Income statements, cash flow statements, balance sheets, general ledger, accounts payable and receivable, for the last five years
    - Credit report
    - Tax returns for at least the past three years
    - Gross profits and rate of return by each product
    - Inventory of all products, equipment, and real estate, including total value

- Business Formation

---

14. Adapted from Bob House, "Due Diligence Checklist—What to Verify Before Buying a Business," BizBuySell (website), https://www.bizbuysell.com/learning-center/article/due-diligence-checklist-what-to-verify-before-buying-a-business.

- Company's articles of incorporation and amendments
- Company's bylaws and amendments
- Summary of current investors and shareholders
- All company names and trademark brand names
- All states where the company is authorized to do business

- Technology

  - Customer demonstration
  - Technical demonstration
  - Patent filings
  - User manuals

- Business Operations

  - All products and services, including production cost and margins
  - Marketing plan, customer analysis, competitors, industry trends
  - Company's brand identity, including logo, website, and domain
  - All customer databases, subscriber lists, and sales records
  - All advertising programs, marketing programs, and events
  - Purchasing policies and refund policies
  - Any customer research data, white papers, or research

- All Contracts

  - Nondisclosure or noncompete agreements, any guarantees
  - Company purchase orders, quotes, invoices, or warranties
  - Security agreements, mortgages, collateral pledges
  - Letters of intent, contracts, closing transcripts from executed mergers or acquisitions
  - Distribution agreements, sales agreements, subscription agreements
  - All loan agreements, material leases, lines of credit, or promissory notes
  - Contracts between officers, directors, or principals of the company
  - Stock-purchase agreements or other options

- Legal and Compliance

  - All attorneys and law firms representing the company, area of practice
  - Pending litigation or threats of litigation
  - Any unsatisfied judgments
  - All insurance coverage and policies
  - All professional licenses and permits
  - All company patents, trademarks, and copyrights
  - Product inventions, formulas, recipes, or technical know-how
  - All rights-owned data and digital information
  - All work-for-hire or consulting agreements
  - Data collection practices
  - Privacy and terms of use

- Human Resources

  - Employee roster and organizational chart
  - Employee contracts and independent contractor agreements
  - Payroll information and employee tax forms
  - Human resources policies and procedures
  - Employee benefits, retirement plan, and insurance

- Anything else that is relevant to someone willing to buy your business

ASK FOR WHAT YOU REALLY WANT

Most importantly, if you find yourself in a situation where you are evaluating buyers' offers, be sure to have prior clarity on exactly what you really want to eventually part from your creation. This business you started and built with lots of hard work, sweat, and tears will only exist once in this configuration. Take the time to undergo a clarity process to ensure you will minimize any possible future seller's remorse. If you are clear on the fact that you are willing to sell your business, then continue your clarity process by focusing on the aspects of an ideal offer. No two acquisition contracts look the same, so get creative about deal terms that meet your goals. Remember, this transaction is only consummated once—so make it count.

GUIDED MEDITATION:
WHAT YOU'D LOVE TO LEAVE BEHIND
———————————————

Take a deep breath, and center yourself inside your body, in the deepest part of your being, where you have the greatest clarity as to who you are.

Impermanence is a consistent and beautiful reminder. All bodies come to an end. All stories come to an end. There's beauty in knowing that this chance is limited, precious, and unique.

With that in mind, how would you like yours to end?

Imagine the best possible ending. What do you see? What do you want to leave behind? Look for sensations and textures, as well as concrete imagery.

How do you want your story to end?

TL;DR

- Attract opportunities by staying visible in very targeted ways and allowing yourself to be found.
- If an opportunity doesn't fully compute, trust that something better can and will come along.
- Keep squeaky-clean financial and formation records.
- Strive for profitability, as this is incredibly attractive to potential acquirers.
- In the face of a dilemma, achieve clarity by conducting a cost/payoff analysis at an emotional, physical, spiritual, and financial level.
- This transaction is only consummated once—so make it count.
- When you build something great, be prepared to let it go. Every masterpiece, whether a business, a piece of art, or a child, will someday need to take on a life of its own.

CLOSING

In January 1939, in Sokolow, Poland, a twenty-six-year-old stocky, short woman named Malke Bekerman found herself up against a frozen wall, held by a Nazi soldier in a stiff gray uniform with swastikas on his sleeve, hat, and lapel.

The soldier reached into his pants pocket, retrieved a pair of sharp scissors, then took those scissors to her long brunette braids, chopping both at the base. The braids fell to the cold concrete like coarsely amputated limbs.

The formula at that time was to live where you were born until the day you died. Malke didn't follow the formula. With trauma still in her body, she boarded a refugee ship and crossed the Atlantic Ocean.

She arrived in Montevideo, Uruguay, with nothing but what she was wearing. Every day, Malke wanted to return to Poland, where at least she spoke the language and knew the people, but returning meant giving up her life—her actual ticking heart. Malke stayed, she worked, she married. And then, in an extremely complicated birth requiring forceps and a vacuum, she gave birth to my father.

My grandmother was an unlikely hero. Her survival instincts are her lavish legacy and the reason I'm alive. When my grandmother chose to forget the formula, and use the resources at her disposal to save her life, she also began to knit a safety net for our family. My parents added stitches to this safety net, via their hard work and further immigration from Uruguay to the United States, making what I've had to "survive" in my life so much easier. Now, here I am. It was my turn to add a few stitches to the safety net, all while not following the formula, all while not *being* the formula.

Stories of people who don't follow the formula, stories of unlikely survivors, are important—they show us what can happen when we refuse to give up, when we blaze trails, when we follow our instincts and receive the gifts of a universe that conspires to help us.

A startup is a difficult endeavor—it is in itself a fight for survival. I believe that those who survive should speak up, so that we can learn the truth: that there's no formula but a million ways to create, succeed, and make an impact.

And so, I end with these wishes for you:

- May you find the inspiration and courage to begin.
- May you transcend the struggle, and create something that aligns with your purpose.
- May you ditch society's labels for gender, race, nationality, age, etc.
- May your startup serve as a vehicle for personal, professional, and financial growth for you and your community.
- May you follow *your* path, the one that's right for you, regardless of whether it's been blazed before.
- May you come to see that there's only one of you in this world, and the world awaits your authentic and valuable creation.

This book is just one story—one founder, one startup, one series of circumstances, one set of lessons.

Keep seeking.

And most important, start living your own startup story.

ACKNOWLEDGMENTS

To my ancestors, Malke Bekerman, Isacc Ryzowy, Ofelia Fojgel, and Mario Zonis, who survived massacres of hate, immigrated to lands unseen, started from scratch, and persevered in peace. To my aunt, Clara Zonis, who helped raise me.

To my father, Walter Ryzowy, whose entrepreneurial spirit mobilized our family from Uruguay to the United States. May you rest in delight, knowing that none of this would've happened had you not chased your American Dream.

To my mother, Olga Ryzowy, whose hardworking and get-stuff-done genes were passed down to me in the most dominant variant, and who inspires me every day to persevere against any and all odds.

To my brothers and their spouses: Javier Ryzowy and Shana Ward Ryzowy for being steady rocks of support and encouragement; Joel and Amanda Ryzowy for their unconditional support and love and their willingness to provide practical connections.

To my extended and supportive family, Esfira Shpilberg, Boris Shpilberg, Moyshe Rekhtman, Shura Rekhtman, Tovah Feldshuh, Andy Levy, Rachel Reyentovich, Irene Piker, Eric Piker, Julia Piker, Nicole Piker, Ida Piker, Yael Ryzowy, Ariel Ryzowy, Yael Rizowy, Michal Rizowy, and Brian Rizowy.

To those who treated me like their own daughter when I needed that most: Pace University professors, Dr. Michael Szenberg and Dr. Ellen Weisbord, my first boss at JP Morgan, Judy Tandon, and Olga Ramirez.

To the Nora crew, Jeff Tong, Mark Joing, Paul Kwon, Jill Giannetonni, Vera Wolowodiuk, Chris McClain, and Chen Yu for providing the starting ground, ample encouragement, and actual work.

To these devoted supporters of Seeker Health without whom this does not compute: Bernard Parker, Diane Weiser, Cory Bartlett, Dave Caponera, Nancy Wilson, Dan Brennan, Vika Boyko, Amy Burroughs, Karen Makhuli, Michael Ward, Sandeep Jutla, Joel Roberts, Jennie Kenyon, Julie Miller, Stacey Harte, Alicia Miller, Andrea Schatz, Yvonne Luu, John Craighead, Hyonelle Johnson, AJ Joshi, John Ditton, Kristin Scott, Charles Wolfus, Silvia Pascual, Dani Heywood, Andrea Johnston, Jason Levin, Renee Gala, Scott Jordan, Ken Martin, Dan Maher, Amy Waterhouse, Bruno Gagnon, Jamie Russo, and Vincent Knobel.

To my board of advisors, Dan Oppenheimer, Barbara Burton, Luke Gelinas, and Kendra Gottlebben. I appreciate your advice—and mostly your open hearts.

To George Buffington and Chris Abato for your legal and diligence support for deal closing.

To Jim Lang, Greg Robitaille, Eric Bishea, Seth Gordon, Tim Guttman, Frank Sterner, Sarah Zwicky, Hebe Berger, Dami Sheppard, Fred Skinner, Franco Spraggins, Dan Bobear, Nicole Pitaniello, Kristin Phillips, Christina Vail, Bill O'Bryon, Megan Jones, Faruk Abdullah, Jodi Ceberio, Jeff Lipman, Herb Lee, Carolyn Quon, and Carol Lam—what a pleasure to cross paths with patient-minded professionals of your caliber and dedication.

To my friends Ilana Lustgarten, Samu Dresel, Iejiel Chilewski, Ethel Berengolc, Claudia Shuster, Rachel Mayer,

Kim Schuy, Nicole Rennie, Patty Wexler, Alicia Saura, Sarah Leshner, Anne Bailey, Caroline Collins, Colleen Morris, Collete Turbeville, Sean Turbeville, Jennette Swartout Leal, Elaine Boxer, Loree Draude, Jenna Fisher, Ramona Persaud, Kara Zubey, Lori Tierney, Julie Lythcott-Haims, Nancy McIntyre, Amy Kacher, Mariana Brandi, Alina Senderzon and Courtney Moore, and to Anya Shapina and Colin Cook for reading an earlier draft.

To my conscious community: Jaime Prieto, Romi Elan, Nancy Larocca Hedley, Dr. Aly Ash, Zahava Griss, Mia Blaisdel, Cindy Nelson, Tilla Torrens, Katt Deschene, and Katya Gogol.

To Charles Rose, my executive coach. The clarity you helped me find was invaluable. Sandra A and Sandra B say thank you for seeing us both.

To the Seeker Health team, past and present, what a privilege to build with you: Vanessa Collado, Debora de Carvalho, Sharon Francis, Nadia Espinoza, Becca Triplett, Heather Hernandez, Kathy Vincent, Amy Ye, Paul Ivsin, Ramesh Samy, Kristina Wolfe, Jenna Villatorro, Ed Decker, Mark Clippinger, Jared Petker, and Mike Kalfus.

To those who helped me get this book in your hands: Annalis Clint and the Girl Friday Productions team of editors, designers, and strategists. Thank you for making this birth beautiful and pain free.

To Phil, my life partner, for sometimes showing me the way, and other times encouraging me to find my own way—and for knowing when to do which. I like how we keep working on our love and our partnership as we grow older together.

To our children, my loves, my life, for participating in this journey—naming my company, designing its logo, naming this book—and absorbing all of it, especially the dinner conversations about EBITDA, valuation multiples, and building something from nothing.

To my own self, for being open to change my mindset, for leaping into the unknown, for integrating my Type A and Type B sides, and for investing the time to share what I've learned.

And finally, to you, for finding this book, or for allowing this book to find you.

WORKS CITED

Bailey, Chris. *Hyperfocus: How to Be More Productive in a World of Distraction*. New York: Viking, 2018.

Bernhard, Toni. *How to Wake Up: A Buddhist-Inspired Guide to Navigating Joy and Sorrow*. Boston: Wisdom Publications, 2013.

Carroll, Ryder. *The Bullet Journal Method: Track the Past, Order the Present, Design the Future*. New York: Portfolio/Penguin, 2018.

Cleveland, Bruce. *Traversing the Traction Gap*. New York: Radius Book Group, 2019.

Duckworth, Angela. *Grit: The Power of Passion and Perseverance*. New York: Scribner, 2016.

Dweck, Carol S. *Mindset: The New Psychology of Success*. New York: Random House, 2006.

Feld, Brad, and Jason Mendelson. *Venture Deals: Be Smarter than Your Lawyer and Venture Capitalist*. Hoboken, NJ: Wiley, 2013.

John, Daymond, and Daniel Paisner. *The Power of Broke: How Empty Pockets, a Tight Budget, and a Hunger for Success Can Become Your Greatest Competitive Advantage*. New York: Crown Business, 2016.

Horowitz, Ben. *The Hard Thing about Hard Things: Building a Business When There Are No Easy Answers*. New York: Harper Business, 2014.

Larkin, Geri. *Plant Seed, Pull Weed: Nurturing the Garden of Your Life*. San Francisco: HarperCollins, 2009.

Manson, Mark. *The Subtle Art of Not Giving a F*ck: A Counterintuitive Approach to Living a Good Life.* New York: HarperCollins, 2016.

Nagoski, Emily, and Amelia Nagoski. *Burnout: The Secret to Unlocking the Stress Cycle.* New York: Ballantine Books, 2019.

Newport, Cal. *Deep Work: Rules for Focused Success in a Distracted World.* New York: Grand Central Publishing, 2016.

Ries, Eric. *The Lean Startup: How Today's Entrepreneurs Use Continuous Innovation to Create Radically Successful Businesses.* New York: Crown Business, 2011.

Seuss, Dr. (Theodor Seuss Geisel). *Oh, the Places You'll Go!* New York: Random House, 1990.

RESOURCES FOR CONTINUED GROWTH

BOOKS

BUSINESS AND STARTUPS

- *Lost and Founder*, Rand Fishkin
- *The Lean Startup*, Eric Ries
- *Crossing the Chasm*, Geoffrey A. Moore
- *Traversing the Traction Gap*, Bruce Cleveland
- *First, Break All the Rules*, Marcus Buckingham
- *Start with Why*, Simon Sinek
- *Startups and Downs*, Mona Bijoor

FUNDING

- *Secrets of Sand Hill Road*, Scott Kupor
- *Venture Deals*, Brad Feld and Jason Mendelson

MINDSET SHIFTERS

- *A Heart as Wide as the World*, Sharon Salzberg
- *Do the Work*, Steven Pressfield
- *Mindset*, Carol Dweck
- *Nonviolent Communication*, Marshall Rosenberg
- *Radical Acceptance*, Tara Brach

- *The Art of Possibility*, Rosamund Stone Zander and Benjamin Zander
- *The Surrender Experiment*, Michael A. Singer
- *When Things Fall Apart*, Pema Chödrön

HEALTHY LIVING

- *Healing with Whole Foods*, Paul Pitchford
- *How Not to Die*, Michael Greger
- *Thrive*, Arianna Huffington
- *Burnout*, Emily Nagoski and Amelia Nagoski

COACHING

- Charles Rose: www.charlesrose.coach

RETREAT CENTERS & RESTORATIVE EVENTS

- Esalen Institute, Big Sur, CA
- 1440 Multiversity, Scotts Valley, CA
- Kripalu Center, Stockbridge, MA
- Omega Institute, Rhinebeck, NY
- Hollyhock, Cortes Island, British Columbia, Canada
- Green Gulch Farm Zen Center, Muir Beach, CA
- Spirit Rock Meditation Center, Woodacre, CA
- Animas Valley Institute, programs worldwide
- Ratna Ling Retreat Center, Cazadero, CA

ADDITIONAL RESOURCES

- Check my website, sandrashpilberg.com, for an evolving and current list of resources for founders.

ABOUT THE AUTHOR

Photo © Lisa DeNeffe

Sandra Shpilberg is the founder and CEO of Seeker Health, a leading digital patient-finding platform. In 2015, Shpilberg founded the company to bring efficiency to the process of finding patients to accelerate the development of treatments for serious diseases. The company grew rapidly to serve sixty-plus biotechnology companies, connect millions of patients with serious diseases to clinical trials, and achieve profitability. In September 2018, a life science services conglomerate acquired Seeker Health. *Medical Marketing & Media* named Sandra Shpilberg a Top 40 Healthcare Transformer, and she was a featured speaker at the 2018 South by Southwest conference and at numerous industry and technology conferences.

Prior to this successful entrepreneurial pursuit, Shpilberg held executive roles at biopharmaceutical companies. She has an MBA in marketing and entrepreneurial management from Wharton School at the University of Pennsylvania.

Shpilberg writes for the *Huffington Post,* and her academic work has been published in *American Economist* and *Lancet.* In addition, Sandra served as editor for *Here My Home Once Stood: A Holocaust Memoir* by Moyshe Rekhtman. Her writing has also been featured in Arianna Huffington's *The Sleep Revolution.*

As an angel investor and startup advisor, Shpilberg invests funds and time to develop the next set of impactful businesses.

She lives with her husband, son, daughter, and shelter dog in Palo Alto, California.

For speaking or advising inquiries, please visit: www.sandrashpilberg.com/contact.